Since he was a young boy, Ruskin Bond has made friends easily. And some of the most rewarding and lasting friendships he has known have been with animals, birds and plants—big and small; outgoing and shy. This collection focuses on these companions and brings together his finest essays and stories, both classic and new. There are leopards and tigers, wise old forest oaks and geraniums on sunny balconies, a talking parrot and a tomcat called Suzie, bears in the mountains and kingfishers in Delhi, a family of langurs and a lonely bat—and many more 'wild' friends, some of an instant, others of several years.

Beautifully illustrated by Shubhadarshini Singh, this is a gift for nature- and book-lovers of all ages.

FRIENDS IN WILD PLACES

FRIENDS IN WILD PLACES

Birds, Beasts and Other Companions

RUSKIN BOND

ILLUSTRATED BY SHUBHADARSHINI SINGH

SPEAKING
TIGER

Speaking Tiger Publishing Pvt. Ltd
4381/4, Ansari Road, Daryaganj,
New Delhi—110002, India

Published in India by Speaking Tiger in hardback 2016
Text copyright © Ruskin Bond 2016
Illustrations copyright © Shubhadarshini Singh 2016

ISBN: 978-93-85755-07-1

eISBN: 978-93-85755-01-9

10 9 8 7 6 5 4 3 2 1

Book design by Tanay Jain

Printed at Gopsons Papers Ltd, Noida

A bird doesn't sing because he has an answer—he sings because he has a song.

—Joan Walsh Anglund

There was room in the world for a mountain lion and me.

—D. H. Lawrence

Contents

Introduction   9

Travelling with Grandfather's Zoo   11

Timothy   18

Adventures in a Banyan Tree   25

A Little World of Mud   33

In the Tunnel   39

The Python   44

The Elephant and the Cassowary Bird   49

Monkey Trouble   52

Harold, Our Hornbill   65

Owls in the Family   70

Uncle Ken's Rumble in the Jungle   73

A Wilderness in Delhi   79

A Year with Suzie   86

My Three Bears   89

A New Flower   94

Our Insect Musicians   97

Birds of the Night   101

To See a Tiger   106

Great Trees I Have Known   113

The Charm of Elephants   122

The Friendship of Flowers   128

Fragrance to the Air   132

The Garden of a Thousand Trees   137

The Silk-Cotton Tree   140

Guests Who Fly in from the Forest   143

No Room for a Leopard   149

Introduction

Most of these stories about birds, animals and insects were written when I was living in Maplewood Lodge, on the outskirts of Mussoorie, some thirty years ago.

Maplewood was a little cottage built into the hillside, and it had stood there for over a hundred years while the forest grew around it. The trees grew close to the old stone walls, and if you opened a window you could step into the branches of a walnut tree or a wild cherry tree. Conversely, any inhabitant of these trees—or the oak and maple trees beside them—could hop in through the window and examine my desk, my books, and my larder. Fortunately the monkeys were not so common or aggressive in those days, and most of my visitors were harmless—beetles, butterflies, moths, a squirrel, a whistling-thrush, a bat, a pair of mynas. And sometimes, in the forest below, a leopard could be heard coughing and moaning in its own peculiar way.

But the leopard did not come in through the window. Leopards usually mind their own business, unless we make life difficult for them—impinge upon their living space or drive away their natural prey.

I wrote about these neighbours of mine, and I also wrote about the Dehradun of my boyhood, then a small town slumbering in a wide green valley. Here my maternal grandfather had built a small house and surrounded it with litchi trees, lemons, mangoes, and papayas, and here he kept various pets from time to time—a tiger cub, a hornbill, a sleepy python—and here I made forays into a banyan tree and a jackfruit tree and others, for there is no limit to the wonderful things you can discover in trees, especially old ones.

And while I was in Maplewood I wrote about all these things. And while I was there I was joined by Prem and his wife and little Rakesh, just a few months old. They came from a remote village in Garhwal. The cottage was kind to us, the forest was friendly. But one day along came the PWD, like an evil giant, and with axes and bulldozers cleared away the forest and built a motor road right under the windows. And the birds and animals retreated into what was left of the forest, down the hill and out of sight, and I had to think of other things to write about.

We moved up the mountain and found more roads, but by then I was getting used to them, and found that I could also write about roads—and how a snail actually managed to cross a busy road without being run over!

Well, the leopards and the wild lilies are long gone, but the stories are still around for you to read, and here are some of them, delightfully illustrated by my good friend Shubhadarshini Singh, who made the charming *Ek Tha Rusty*, a TV serial, some years ago.

Ruskin Bond
Landour, Mussoorie
September, 2015

Travelling with Grandfather's Zoo

'ALL ABOARD!' shrieked Popeye, Grandmother's pet parrot, as the family climbed aboard the Lucknow Express. We were moving for some months from Dehra to Lucknow, and as Grandmother had insisted on taking her parrot along, Grandfather and I insisted on bringing our pets too—a teenaged tiger (Grandfather's) and a small squirrel (mine). But we thought it prudent to leave the python behind.

In those days trains in India were not so crowded and it was possible to travel with a variety of creatures. Grandfather had decided to do things in style by travelling first-class, so we had a four-berth compartment of our own, and Timothy, the tiger, had an entire berth to himself. Later, everyone agreed that Timothy behaved perfectly throughout the journey. Even the guard admitted that he could not have asked for a better passenger: no stealing from vendors, no shouting at coolies, no breaking of railway property, no spitting on the platform.

All the same, the journey was not without incident and before we reached Lucknow, there was excitement enough for everyone.

To begin with, Popeye objected to vendors and other people poking their hands in through the windows. Before the train had moved out of Dehra station, he had nipped two fingers and tweaked a ticket inspector's ear.

No sooner had the train started moving than Chips, my squirrel, emerged from my pocket to examine his surroundings. Before I could stop him, he was out of the compartment door, scurrying along the corridor.

Chips discovered that the train was a squirrel's paradise, almost all the passengers having bought large quantities of roasted peanuts before the train pulled out. He had no difficulty in making friends with both children and grown-ups, and it was an hour before he returned to our compartment, his tummy almost bursting.

'I think I'll go to sleep,' said Grandmother, covering herself with a blanket and stretching out on the berth opposite Timothy's. 'It's been a tiring day.'

'Aren't you going to eat anything?' asked Grandfather.

'I'm not hungry—I had some soup before we left. You two help yourselves from the tiffin basket.'

Grandmother dozed off, and even Popeye started nodding, lulled to sleep by the clackety-clack of the wheels and the steady puffing of the steam engine.

'Well, I'm hungry,' I said. 'What did Granny make for us?'

'Ham sandwiches, boiled eggs, a roast chicken, gooseberry pie. It's all in the tiffin basket under your berth.'

I tugged at the large basket and dragged it into the centre of the compartment. The straps were loosely tied. No sooner had I undone them than the lid flew open, and I let out a gasp of surprise.

In the basket was Grandfather's pet python, curled up contentedly on the remains of our dinner. Grandmother had insisted that we leave the python behind, and Grandfather had let it loose in the garden. Somehow, it had managed to snuggle itself into the tiffin basket.

'Well, what are you staring at?' asked Grandfather from his corner.

'It's the python,' I said. 'And it has finished all our dinner.'

Grandfather joined me, and together we looked down at what remained of the food. Pythons don't chew, they swallow: outlined along the length of the large snake's sleek body were the distinctive shapes of a chicken, a pie and six boiled eggs. We couldn't make out the ham sandwiches, but presumably these had been eaten too because there was no sign of them in the basket. Only a few apples remained. Evidently, the python did not care for apples.

Grandfather snapped the basket shut and pushed it back beneath the berth.

'We mustn't let Grandmother see him,' he said. 'She might think we brought him along on purpose.'

'Well, I'm hungry,' I complained. Just then, Chips returned from one of his forays and presented me with a peanut.

'Thanks,' I said. 'If you keep bringing me peanuts all night, I might last until morning.'

But it was not long before I felt sleepy. Grandfather had begun to nod and the only one who was wide awake was the squirrel, still intent on investigating distant compartments.

A little after midnight there was a great clamour at the end of the corridor. Grandfather and I woke up. Timothy growled in his sleep, and Popeye made complaining noises.

Suddenly there were cries of 'Saap, saap!' (Snake, snake!)

Grandfather was on his feet in a moment. He looked under the berth. The tiffin basket was empty.

'The python's out,' he said, and dashed out of our compartment in his pyjamas. I was close behind.

About a dozen passengers were bunched together outside the washroom door.

'Anything wrong?' asked Grandfather casually.

'We can't get into the toilet,' said someone. 'There's a huge snake inside.'

'Let me take a look,' said Grandfather. 'I know all about snakes.'

The passengers made way for him, and he entered the washroom to find the python curled up in the washbasin. After its heavy meal it had become thirsty and, finding the lid of the tiffin basket easy to pry up, had set out in search of water.

Grandfather gathered up the sleepy, overfed python and stepped out of the washroom. The passengers hastily made way for them.

'Nothing to worry about,' said Grandfather cheerfully. 'It's just a harmless young python. He's had his dinner already, so no one is in any danger!' And he marched back to our compartment with the python in his arms. As soon as I was inside, he bolted the door.

Grandmother was sitting up on her berth.

'I knew you'd do something foolish behind my back,' she scolded. 'You told me you'd got rid of that creature, and all the time you've been hiding it from me.'

Grandfather tried to explain that we had nothing to do with it, that the python had smuggled itself into the tiffin basket, but Grandmother was unconvinced. 'What will Mabel do when she sees it!' she cried despairingly.

My Aunt Mabel was a schoolteacher in Lucknow. She was going to share our new house, and she was terrified of all reptiles, particularly snakes.

'We won't let her see it,' said Grandfather. 'Back it goes into the tiffin basket.'

Early next morning, the train steamed into Lucknow. Aunt Mabel was on the platform to receive us.

Grandfather let all the other passengers get off before he emerged from the compartment with Timothy on a chain. I had Chips in my pocket, suitcase in both hands. Popeye stayed perched on Grandmother's shoulder, eyeing the busy platform with considerable distrust.

Aunt Mabel, a lover of good food, immediately spotted the tiffin basket, picked it up and said, 'It's not very heavy. I'll carry it out to the taxi. I hope you've kept something for me.'

'A whole chicken,' I said.

'We hardly ate anything,' said Grandfather.

'It's all yours, Aunty!' I added.

'Oh, good!' exclaimed Aunt Mabel. 'It's been ages since I tasted something cooked by your grandmother.' And after that there was no getting the basket away from her.

Glancing at it, I thought I saw the lid bulging, but Grandfather had tied it down quite firmly this time and there was little likelihood of its suddenly bursting open.

An enormous 1950 Chevrolet taxi was waiting outside the station, and the family tumbled into it. Timothy got onto the back seat, leaving enough room for Grandfather and me. Aunt Mabel sat in front with Grandmother, the tiffin basket on her lap.

'Tell the taxi driver where to take us, dear,' said Grandmother. 'He's looking rather nervous.'

Aunt Mabel gave instructions to the driver and the taxi shot off in a cloud of dust.

'Well, here we go!' said Grandfather. 'I'm looking forward to settling into the new house.'

Popeye, perched proudly on Grandmother's shoulder, kept one suspicious eye on the quivering tiffin basket.

'All aboard!' he squawked. 'All aboard!'

When we got to our new house, we found a light breakfast waiting for us on the dining table.

'It isn't much,' said Aunt Mabel. 'But we'll supplement it with the contents of your hamper.' And placing the basket on the table, she removed the lid.

The python was half-asleep, with an apple in its mouth. Aunt Mabel was no Eve, to be tempted. She fainted away.

Grandfather promptly picked up the python, took it into the garden, and draped it over a branch of a guava tree.

When Aunt Mabel recovered, she insisted that there was a huge snake in the tiffin basket. We showed her the empty basket.

'You're seeing things,' said Grandfather.

'It must be the heat,' I said.

Grandmother said nothing. But Popeye broke into shrieks of maniacal laughter, and soon everyone, including a slightly hysterical Aunt Mabel, was doubled up with laughter.

Timothy

TIMOTHY, THE tiger cub, was discovered by Grandfather on a hunting expedition in the Terai jungle near Dehra.

Grandfather was no shikari, but as he knew the forests of the Siwalik hills better than most people, he was persuaded to accompany the party—it consisted of several Very Important Persons from Delhi—to advise on the terrain and the direction the beaters should take once a tiger had been spotted.

The camp itself was sumptuous—seven large tents (one for each shikari), a dining-tent, and a number of servants' tents. The dinner was very good, as Grandfather admitted afterwards; it was not often that one saw hot-water plates, finger-glasses, and seven or eight courses, in a tent in the jungle! But that was how things were done in the days of the Viceroys. . .There were also some fifteen elephants, four of them with howdahs for the shikaris, and the others specially trained for taking part in the beat.

The sportsmen never saw a tiger, nor did they shoot anything else, though they saw a number of deer, peacocks, and wild boars. They were giving up all hope of finding a tiger, and were beginning to shoot at jackals, when Grandfather, strolling down the forest path at some distance from the rest of the party, discovered a little tiger about 18 inches long, hiding among the intricate roots of a banyan tree. Grandfather picked him up, and brought him home after the camp had broken up. He had the distinction of being the only member of the party to have bagged any game, dead or alive.

At first the tiger cub, who was named Timothy by Grandmother, was brought up entirely on milk given to him in a feeding bottle by our cook, Mahmoud. But the milk proved too rich for him, and he was put on a diet of raw mutton and cod liver oil, to be followed later by a more tempting diet of pigeons and rabbits.

Timothy was provided with two companions—Toto the monkey, who was bold enough to pull the young tiger by the tail, and then climb up the curtains if Timothy lost his temper; and a small mongrel puppy, found on the road by Grandfather.

At first Timothy appeared to be quite afraid of the puppy, and darted back with a spring if it came too near. He would make absurd dashes at it with his large forepaws, and then retreat to a ridiculously safe distance. Finally, he allowed the puppy to crawl on his back and rest there!

One of Timothy's favourite amusements was to stalk anyone who would play with him, and so, when I came to live with Grandfather, I became one of the favourites of the tiger. With a crafty look in his glittering eyes, and his body crouching, he would creep closer and closer to me, suddenly making a dash for my feet, rolling over on his back and kicking me in delight, and pretending to bite my ankles.

He was by this time the size of a full-grown retriever, and when I took him out for walks, people on the road would give us a wide berth. When he pulled hard on his chain, I had difficulty in keeping up with him. His favourite place in the house was the drawing room, and he would make himself comfortable on the long sofa, reclining there with great dignity, and snarling at anybody who tried to get him off.

Timothy had clean habits, and would scrub his face with his paws exactly like a cat. He slept at night in the cook's quarters, and was always delighted at being let out by him in the morning.

'One of these days,' declared Grandmother in her prophetic manner, 'we are going to find Timothy sitting on Mahmoud's bed, and no sign of the cook except his clothes and shoes!'

Of course, it never came to that, but when Timothy was about six months old a change came over him; he grew steadily less friendly. When out for a walk with me, he would try to steal away to stalk a cat or someone's pet Pekinese. Sometimes at night we would hear frenzied cackling from the poultry house, and in the morning there would be feathers lying all over the veranda. Timothy had to be chained up more often. And finally, when he began to stalk Mahmoud about the house with what looked like villainous intent, Grandfather decided it was time to transfer him to a zoo.

The nearest zoo was at Lucknow, 200 miles away. Reserving a first-class compartment for himself and Timothy—no one would share a compartment with them—Grandfather took him to Lucknow where the zoo authorities were only too glad to receive as a gift a well-fed and fairly civilized tiger.

About six months later, when my grandparents were visiting their relatives in Lucknow, Grandfather took the opportunity of calling at the zoo to see how Timothy was getting on. I was not there to accompany him, but I heard all about it when he returned to Dehra.

Arriving at the zoo, Grandfather made straight for the particular cage in which Timothy had been interned. The tiger was there, crouched in a corner, full-grown and with a magnificent striped coat.

'Hello Timothy!' said Grandfather, and, climbing the railing with ease, he put his arm through the bars of the cage.

The tiger approached the bars, and allowed Grandfather to put both hands around his head. Grandfather stroked the tiger's forehead and tickled his ear, and whenever he growled, smacked him across the mouth, which was his old way of keeping him quiet.

He licked Grandfather's hands and only sprang away when a leopard in the next cage snarled at him. Grandfather 'shooed' the leopard away, and the tiger returned to lick his hands; but every now and then the leopard would rush at the bars, and the tiger would slink back to his corner.

A number of people had gathered to watch the reunion when a keeper pushed his way through the crowd and asked Grandfather what he was doing. 'I'm talking to Timothy,' said Grandfather. 'Weren't you here when I gave him to the zoo six months ago?'

'I haven't been here very long,' said the surprised keeper. 'Please continue your conversation. But I have never been able to touch him myself, he is always very bad tempered.'

'Why don't you put him somewhere else?' suggested Grandfather. 'That leopard keeps frightening him. I'll go and see the Superintendent about it.'

Grandfather went in search of the Superintendent of the zoo, but found that he had gone home early; and so, after wandering about the zoo for a little while, he returned to Timothy's cage to say goodbye. It was beginning to get dark.

He had been stroking and slapping Timothy for about five minutes when he found another keeper observing him with some alarm. Grandfather recognized him as the keeper who had been there when Timothy had first come to the zoo.

'You remember me,' said Grandfather. 'Now why don't you transfer Timothy to another cage, away from this stupid leopard?'

'But—sir—' stammered the keeper, 'it is not your tiger.'

'I know, I know,' said Grandfather testily. 'I realize he is no longer mine. But you might at least take a suggestion or two from me.'

'I remember your tiger very well,' said the keeper. 'He died two months ago.'

'Died!' exclaimed Grandfather.

'Yes, sir, of pneumonia. This tiger was trapped in the hills only last month, and he is very dangerous!' Grandfather could think of nothing to say. The tiger was still licking his arm, with increasing relish. Grandfather took what seemed to him an age to withdraw his hand from the cage.

With his face near the tiger's he mumbled, 'Goodnight, Timothy,' and giving the keeper a scornful look, walked briskly out of the zoo.

Adventures in a Banyan Tree

DEHRA WAS a good place for trees, and Grandfather's house was surrounded by several kinds—peepul, neem, mango, jackfruit and papaya. There was also an ancient banyan tree. Though the house and grounds were Grandfather's domain, the magnificent old banyan tree was mine—chiefly because Grandfather, at the age of 65, could no longer climb it. Grandmother used to tease him about this, and would speak of a certain Countess of Desmond, an Englishwoman who lived to the age of 117, and would have lived longer if she hadn't fallen while climbing an apple tree.

The spreading branches of the banyan tree, which curved to the ground and took root again, forming a maze of arches, gave me endless pleasure. The tree was older than the house, older than Grandfather, as old as the town of Dehra, nestling in a valley at the foot of the Himalayas. And this old, old tree became my favourite haunt. I could hide myself in its branches, behind thick green leaves, and spy on the world below.

My first friend and familiar there was a small grey squirrel. Arching his back and sniffing into the air, he seemed at first to resent my invasion of his privacy. But, when he found that I did not arm myself with a catapult or an air-gun, he became friendlier. And, when I started leaving him pieces of cake and biscuit, he grew bolder, and finally became familiar enough to take food from my hands.

Before long he was delving into my pockets and helping himself to whatever he could find. He was a very young squirrel, and his friends and relatives probably thought him headstrong and foolish for trusting a human.

In the spring, when the banyan tree was full of small red figs, birds of all kinds would flock into its branches, the red-bottomed bulbul, cheerful and greedy; gossiping rosy-pastors; and parrots and crows, squabbling with each other all the time. During the fig season, the banyan tree was the noisiest place on the road.

Halfway up the tree I had built a small platform on which I would often spend the afternoons when it wasn't too hot. I could read there, propping myself up against the bole of the tree with cushions taken from the drawing room. *Treasure Island, Huck Finn,* the *Mowgli Stories,* and the novels of Edgar Wallace, Edgar Rice Burroughs and Louisa May Alcott made up my bag of very mixed reading.

When I didn't want to read, I could look down through the banyan leaves at the world below, at Grandmother hanging up or taking down the washing, at the cook quarrelling with a fruit vendor or at Grandfather grumbling at the hardy Indian marigolds which insisted on springing up all over his very English garden. Usually nothing very exciting happened while I was in the banyan tree, but on one particular afternoon I had enough excitement to last me through the summer.

That was the time I saw a mongoose and a cobra fight to death in the garden, while I sat directly above them in the banyan tree.

It was an April afternoon. And the warm breezes of approaching summer had sent everyone, including Grandfather, indoors. I was feeling drowsy myself and was wondering if I should go to the pond behind the house for a swim, when I saw a huge black cobra gliding out of a clump of cactus and making for some cooler part of the garden. At the same time a mongoose (whom I had often seen) emerged from the bushes and went straight for the cobra.

In a clearing beneath the tree, in bright sunshine, they came face to face.

The cobra knew only too well that the grey mongoose, three feet long, was a superb fighter, clever and aggressive. But the cobra was a skilful and experienced fighter too. He could move swiftly and strike with the speed of light, and the sacs behind his long, sharp fangs were full of deadly venom.

It was to be a battle of champions.

Hissing defiance, his forked tongue darting in and out, the cobra raised three of his six feet off the ground, and spread his broad, spectacled hood. The mongoose bushed his tail. The long hair on his spine stood up (in the past, the very thickness of his hair had saved him from bites that would have been fatal to others).

Though the combatants were unaware of my presence in the banyan tree, they soon became aware of the arrival of two other spectators. One was a myna, and the other a jungle crow (not the wily urban crow). They had seen these preparations for battle, and had settled on the cactus to watch the outcome. Had they been content only to watch, all would have been well with both of them.

The cobra stood on the defensive, swaying slowly from side to side, trying to mesmerize the mongoose into making a false move. But the mongoose knew the power of his opponent's glassy, unwinking eyes, and refused to meet them. Instead he fixed his gaze at a point just below the cobra's hood, and opened the attack.

Moving forward quickly until he was just within the cobra's reach, he made a feint to one side. Immediately the cobra struck. His great hood came down so swiftly that I thought nothing could save the mongoose. But the little fellow jumped neatly to one side, and darted in as swiftly as the cobra, biting the snake on the back and darting away again out of reach.

The moment the cobra struck, the crow and the myna hurled themselves at him, only to collide heavily in mid-air. Shrieking at each other, they returned to the cactus plant.

A few drops of blood glistened on the cobra's back.

The cobra struck again and missed. Again the mongoose sprang aside, jumped in and bit. Again the birds dived at the snake, bumped into each other instead, and returned shrieking to the safety of the cactus.

The third round followed the same course as the first but with one dramatic difference. The crow and the myna, still determined to take part in the proceedings, dived at the cobra, but this time they missed each other as well as their mark. The myna flew on and reached its perch, but the crow tried to pull up in mid-air and turn back. In the second that it took him to do this, the cobra whipped his head back and struck with great force, his snout thudding against the crow's body.

I saw the bird flung nearly 20 feet across the garden, where, after fluttering about for a while, it lay still. The myna remained on the cactus plant, and when the snake and the mongoose returned to the fray, it very wisely refrained from interfering again!

The cobra was weakening, and the mongoose, walking fearlessly up to it, raised himself on his short legs, and with a lightning snap had the big snake by the snout. The cobra writhed and lashed about in a frightening manner, and even coiled itself about the mongoose, but all to no avail. The little fellow hung grimly on, until the snake had ceased to struggle. He then smelt along its quivering length, and gripping it round the hood, dragged it into the bushes.

The myna dropped cautiously to the ground, hopped about, peered into the bushes from a safe distance, and then, with a shrill cry of congratulation, flew away.

When I had also made a cautious descent from the tree and returned to the house, I told Grandfather of the fight I had seen. He was pleased that the mongoose had won. He had encouraged it to live in the garden, to keep away the snakes, and fed it regularly with scraps from the kitchen. He had never tried

taming it, because a wild mongoose was more useful than a domesticated one.

From the banyan tree I often saw the mongoose patrolling the four corners of the garden, and once I saw him with an egg in his mouth and knew he had been in the poultry house; but he hadn't harmed the birds, and I knew Grandmother would forgive him for stealing as long as he kept the snakes away from the house.

The banyan tree was also the setting for what we were to call the Strange Case of the Grey Squirrel and the White Rat.

The white rat was Grandfather's—he had bought it from the bazaar for four annas—but I would often take it with me into the banyan tree, where it soon struck up a friendship with one of the squirrels. They would go off together on little excursions among the roots and branches of the old tree.

Then the squirrel started building a nest. At first she tried building it in my pockets, and when I went indoors and changed my clothes I would find straw and grass falling out. Then one day Grandmother's knitting was missing. We hunted for it everywhere but without success.

Next day I saw something glinting in the hole in the banyan tree and, going up to investigate, saw that it was the end of Grandmother's steel knitting-needle. On looking further, I discovered that the hole was crammed with knitting. And amongst the wool were three baby squirrels—all of them white!

Grandfather had never seen white squirrels before, and we gazed at them in wonder. We were puzzled for some time, but when I mentioned the white rat's frequent visits to the tree, Grandfather told me that the rat must be the father. Rats and squirrels were related to each other, he said, and so it was quite possible for them to have offspring—in this case, white squirrels!

There were little adventures happening in the banyan tree through the year; one only had to look and listen. It was a world in itself, populated with many small beasts and large insects. While the banyan's leaves were still pink and tender, they would be visited by the delicate map butterfly, who committed her eggs to their care. The 'honey' on the leaves—an edible smear—also attracted the little striped squirrels. Redheaded parakeets swarmed about the tree early in the mornings.

But the banyan really came to life during the monsoon, when the branches were thick with scarlet figs. These berries were not fit for human consumption, but the many birds that gathered in the tree—gossipy rosy pastors, quarrelsome mynas, cheerful bulbuls and coppersmiths, and sometimes a raucous, bullying crow—feasted on them. And when night fell, and the birds were resting, the dark flying foxes flapped heavily about the tree, chewing and munching as they clambered over the branches.

Yes, the banyan tree was a noisy place during the rains. If the brainfever bird made music by night, the crickets and cicadas orchestrated during the day. As musicians, the cicadas were in a class by themselves. All through the hot weather their chorus rang through the garden, while a shower of rain, far from damping their spirits,

only roused them to a greater choral effort.

The tree crickets were a band of willing artists who commenced their performance at almost any time of the day but preferably in the evenings. Delicate pale green creatures with transparent green wings, they were hard to find amongst the lush monsoon foliage; but once located, a tap on the bush or leaf on which they sat would put an immediate end to the performance.

At the height of the monsoon, the banyan tree was like an orchestra pit with the musicians constantly tuning up. Birds, insects and squirrels expressed their joy at the termination of the hot weather and the cool quenching relief of the monsoon.

A toy flute in my hands, I would try adding my shrill piping to theirs. But they thought poorly of my musical ability. Whenever I piped, the birds and the insects fell into a pained and puzzled silence.

A Little World of Mud

I **HAD** never imagined there was much to be found in the rainwater pond behind our house in Dehra except for large quantities of mud and some-times a water-buffalo. It was Grandfather who introduced me to the pond's diversity of life, so beautifully arranged that each individual gained some benefit from the well-being of the mass. To the inhabitants of the pond, the pond was the world; and to the inhabitants of the world, maintained Grandfather, the world was but a muddy pond.

When Grandfather first showed me the pond world, he chose a dry place in the shade of an old peepul tree, where we sat for an hour, gazing steadily at the thin, green scum on the water. The buffaloes had not arrived for their afternoon dip, and the surface of the pond was still. For the first ten minutes we saw noth-ing. Then a small black blob appeared in the middle of the pond; gradually it rose higher, until at last we could make out a frog's head, its great eyes staring hard at us. He did not know if we were friend or enemy and kept his body out of sight. A heron, his mortal enemy, might have been wading about in search of him. When he had made sure we were not herons, he informed his friends and neighbours, and soon there were several big heads and eyes just above the surface of the water. Throats swelled, and a wurk, wurk, wurk began.

In the shallow water near the tree we could see a dark shifting shadow. When touched with the end of a stick, the dark mass immediately became alive. Thousands of little black tadpoles wriggled into life, pushing and hustling each other.

'What do tadpoles eat?' I asked.

'They eat each other most of the time,' said Grandfather. 'It may seem an unpleasant custom, but when you think of the thousands of tadpoles that are hatched, you'll realize what a useful system it is. If all the young tadpoles in this pond became frogs, they'd take up every inch of ground between here and the house!'

'Their croaking would certainly drive Grandmother crazy,' I said.

All the same, I took home a number of frogs, placed them in a large glass jar, and left them on the window-sill of my bedroom.

At about four o'clock in the morning the entire household was awakened by a loud and fearful noise, and my grandparents, aunts and servants gathered on the veranda for safety. They were furious when they discovered that my frogs were the cause of the noise. Seeing the dawn breaking, the frogs had with one accord begun their morning song. Grandmother wanted to throw the frogs, bottle and all, out of the window; but Grandfather gave

the bottle a good shaking and the frogs stayed quiet. Everyone went back to bed, but I was obliged to stay awake, to shake the bottle whenever the frogs showed signs of bursting into song. Long before breakfast, I had let them loose in the garden.

I was soon visiting the pond on my own, exploring its banks and shallows; and taking off my shoes, I would wade into the muddy water up to my knees, and pluck the water-lilies floating on the surface.

One day, when I reached the pond, I found it occupied by buffaloes. Their owner, a boy a little older than me, was swimming about in the middle of the pond. He pulled himself up on the back of one of his buffaloes, stretched his slim brown body out on the animal's glistening back, and started singing to himself.

When the boy saw me staring at him, he smiled, showing gleaming white teeth in his dark, sun-burnished face. He invited me into the water for a swim. I told him I couldn't swim, and he offered to teach me. I hesitated, knowing that my Grandmother held strict and rather old-fashioned views about my mixing with village children; but, deciding that Grandfather—who sometimes smoked a hookah on the sly—would get me out of any trouble that might arise, I took the bold step of accepting the boy's offer. And once taken, the step did not seem so very bold.

He dived off the back of his buffalo and swam across to me. And I, having removed my shirt and shorts, followed his instructions until I was floundering about among the water-lilies. His name was Ramu, and he promised to give me swimming lessons every afternoon; and so it was during the afternoons—especially summer afternoons when everyone was asleep—that we met.

Before long I was able to swim across the pond to sit with Ramu astride a contented buffalo standing like an island in the middle of a muddy ocean. Sometimes we would try racing the buffaloes, Ramu and I sitting on different beasts. But they

were lazy creatures and would leave one comfortable spot only to look for another; or, if they were in no mood for games, would simply roll over on their backs, taking us with them into the mud and green slime of the pond. I would emerge from the pond in shades of green and khaki, slip into the house through the bathroom, and bathe under the tap before getting into my clothes.

Ramu came from a family of low-caste farmers and had received no schooling. But he was well versed in folklore and knew a great deal about birds and animals.

'Many birds are sacred,' he told me, as a blue jay swooped down from the peepul tree and carried off a grasshopper. Ramu said that both the blue jay and the god Shiva were called Nilkanth. Shiva had a blue throat, like the bird, because out of compassion for the human race he had swallowed a deadly poison which was meant to destroy the world. Keeping the poison in his throat, he had not let it go further.

'Are squirrels sacred?' I asked.

'The god Krishna loved them,' said Ramu. He would take them in his arms and stroke them with his long fingers. That is why they have four dark lines down their back from head to tail. Krishna was very dark, and the lines are the marks of his fingers.'

Both Ramu and my grandfather felt that we should be more gentle with birds and animals, that we should not kill them indiscriminately.

'We must acknowledge their rights on the earth,' said Grandfather. 'Everywhere, birds and animals are finding it more difficult to live, because we are destroying their forests. They have to keep moving as the trees disappear.'

Ramu and I spent many long summer afternoons at the pond. We never saw each other again after I left my grandparents' house; he could not read or write, so we were unable to keep in touch.

No one knew of our friendship. Only the buffaloes and the frogs were our confidants. They had accepted us as part of their own world, their muddy but comfortable pond. And when I went away, both they and Ramu must have assumed that I would return again like the birds.

In the Tunnel

THE FIRST time I saw a train, I was standing on a wooded slope outside a tunnel, not far from Kalka. Suddenly, with a shrill whistle and great burst of steam, a green and black engine came snorting out of the blackness.

I turned and ran to my father. 'A dragon!' I shouted. 'There's a dragon coming out of its cave!'

Since then, steam engines and dragons have always inspired the same sort of feelings in me—wonder and awe and delight. I would like to see a real dragon one day, green and gold and—because I have always preferred the 'reluctant' sort—rather shy and gentle; but until that day comes, I shall be content with steam engines.

In India the steam engine is still very much with us. In 1885 the East India Railway was opened between Calcutta and Raniganj, a distance of 122 miles. By the turn of the century, India had one of the most extensive railway systems in the world. Today, the hundreds of trains that criss-cross the subcontinent, panting over the desert and plain, through hill and forest, are still pulled by these snorting monsters who belch smoke by day and scatter red stars in the night.

Even now, when I see a train coming around the bend of a hill, on crossing a bridge, or cutting across a wide flat plain, I feel the same sort of innocent wonder that I felt as a boy. Where are all these people going to, and where have they come from, and what are they really like? When children wave to me from

carriage windows I wave back to them. It is a habit I have never lost. And sometimes I am in a train, waving, and the children from the nearby villages come running out of their mud huts to wave back to me—well, not to me exactly, it is really the train they are waving to. . .

Small wayside stations have always fascinated me. Manned sometimes by just one or two railway employees, and often situated in the middle of a damp subtropical forest, or clinging to the mountainside on the way to Simla or Darjeeling, these little stations are, for me, outposts of romance, lonely symbols of the pioneering spirit that led men to lay tracks into the remote corners of the earth.

I remember such a stop on a line that went through the Terai forests near the foothills of the Himalayas. At about ten at night, the khilasi, or station watchman, lit his kerosene lamp and started walking up the tracks into the jungle.

'Where are you going?' I asked.

'To see if the tunnel is clear,' he said. 'The Overland Mail comes in twenty minutes.'

I accompanied him a furlong or two along the track, through a deep cutting which led to the tunnel. Every night, the khilasi walked through the dark tunnel, and then stood outside to wave his lamp to the oncoming train as a signal that the track was clear. If the engine driver did not see the lamp he stopped the train. It always slowed down near the cutting.

Having inspected the tunnel, we stood outside, waiting for the train. It seemed a long time coming. There was no moon, and the dense forest seemed to be trying to crowd us into the narrow cutting. The sounds of the forest came to us—the belling of a sambhur deer and the cry of a jackal told us that perhaps a tiger or a leopard was on the prowl. There were strange, nocturnal bird sounds; and then silence.

The khilasi stood outside the tunnel, trimming his lamp, listening to the faint sounds of the jungle—sounds which only he could identify and understand. Something made him stand very still for a few moments, peering into the darkness, and I knew that everything was not as it should be.

'There is something in the tunnel,' he said.

I could hear nothing at first, but then there came a regular sawing sound, just like the sound made by someone sawing through the branch of a tree.

'Baghera!' whispered the khilasi. He had said enough to enable me to recognize the sound—the sawing of a leopard trying to find its mate. 'The train will be coming soon. We must drive the animal out, or it will be run over!'

He must have sensed my surprise, because he said, 'Do not be afraid...I know this leopard well. We have seen each other many times. He has a weakness for stray dogs and goats, but he will not harm us.' He gave me his small handaxe to hold and, raising his lamp high, started walking into the tunnel, shouting at the top of his voice to try and scare away the animal. I followed close behind him.

We had gone about 20 yards into the tunnel when the light from the lamp fell on the leopard, which was crouching between the tracks, only about 20 feet away from us. It bared its teeth in a snarl and went down on its stomach, tail twisting. I thought it was going to spring. The khilasi and I both shouted together. Our voices rang and echoed through the tunnel. And the leopard, uncertain as to how many humans were in there with him, turned swiftly and disappeared into the darkness ahead.

The khilasi and I walked on till the end of the tunnel without seeing the leopard again. As we returned to the entrance of the tunnel the rails began to hum and we knew the train was coming.

I put my hand to one of the rails and felt its tremor. And then the engine came round the bend, hissing at us, scattering sparks into the darkness, defying the jungle as it roared through the steep sides of the cutting. It charged straight at the tunnel and into it, thundering past us like the beautiful dragon of my dreams.

And when it had gone, the silence returned and the forest breathed again. Only the rails still trembled with the passing of the train.

The Python

WHEN GRANDFATHER brought home a python, Grandmother was not amused. She was tolerant of most birds and many animals, but she drew the line at reptiles. She said they made her blood run cold. Even a handsome, sweet-tempered chameleon had to be given up. Grandfather should have known that there was little chance of his being allowed to keep the python. It was about four feet long, a young one, when Grandfather bought it from a snake charmer for six rupees, impressing the bazaar crowd by slinging it across his shoulders and walking home with it. Grandmother nearly fainted at the sight of the python curled round Grandfather's throat.

'You'll be strangled!' she cried. 'Get rid of it at once!'

'Nonsense,' said Grandfather. 'He's only a young fellow. He'll soon get used to us.'

'Will he, indeed?' said Grandmother. 'But I have no intention of getting used to him. You know quite well that your cousin Mabel is coming to stay with us tomorrow. She'll leave us the minute she knows there's a snake in the house.'

'Well, perhaps we ought to show it to her as soon as she arrives,' said Grandfather, who did not look forward to fussy Aunt Mabel's visits any more than I did.

'You'll do no such thing,' said Grandmother.

'Well, I can't let it loose in the garden,' said Grandfather with an innocent expression. 'It might find its way into the poultry house, and then where would we be?'

'How exasperating you are!' grumbled Grandmother. 'Lock the creature in the bathroom, go back to the bazaar and find the man you bought it from, and get him to come and take it back.'

In my awestruck presence, Grandfather had to take the python into the bathroom, where he placed it in a steep-sided tin tub. Then he hurried off to the bazaar to look for the snake charmer, while Grandmother paced anxiously up and down the veranda. When he returned looking crestfallen, we knew he hadn't been able to find the man.

'You had better take it away yourself,' said Grandmother, in a relentless mood. 'Leave it in the jungle across the river bed.'

'All right, but let me give it a feed first', said Grandfather; and producing a plucked chicken, he took it into the bathroom, followed, in single file, by me, Grandmother, and a curious cook and gardener.

Grandfather threw open the door and stepped into the bathroom. I peeped round his legs, while the others remained well behind. We couldn't see the python anywhere.

'He's gone,' announced Grandfather. 'He must have felt hungry.'

'I hope he isn't too hungry,' I said.

'We left the window open,' said Grandfather, looking embarrassed.

A careful search was made of the house, the kitchen, the garden, the stable and the poultry shed; but the python couldn't be found anywhere.

'He'll be well away by now,' said Grandfather reassuringly.

'I certainly hope so,' said Grandmother, who was half way between anxiety and relief.

Aunt Mabel arrived next day for a three-week visit, and for a couple of days Grandfather and I were a little apprehensive in case the python made a sudden reappearance, but on the third day, when he didn't show up, we felt confident that he had gone for good.

And then, towards evening, we were startled by a scream from the garden. Seconds later, Aunt Mabel came flying up the veranda steps, looking as though she had seen a ghost.

'In the guava tree!' she gasped. 'I was reaching for a guava, when I saw it staring at me. The look in its eyes! As though it would devour me—'

'Calm down, my dear,' urged Grandmother, sprinkling her with eau-de-cologne. 'Calm down and tell us what you saw.'

'A snake!' sobbed Aunt Mabel. 'A great boa constrictor. It must have been twenty feet long! In the guava tree. Its eyes were terrible. It looked at me in such a queer way...'

My grandparents looked significantly at each other, and Grandfather said, 'I'll go out and kill it,' and sheepishly taking hold of an umbrella, sallied out into the garden. But when he reached the guava tree, the python had disappeared.

'Aunt Mabel must have frightened it away,' I said.

'Hush,' said Grandfather. 'We mustn't speak of your aunt in that way.' But his eyes were alive with laughter.

After this incident, the python began to make a series of appearances, often in the most unexpected places. Aunt Mabel had another fit of hysterics when she saw him admiring her from under a cushion. She packed her bags, and Grandmother made us intensify the hunt.

Next morning, I saw the python curled up on the dressing table, gazing at his reflection in the mirror. I went for Grandfather, but by the time we returned, the python had moved elsewhere. A little later he was seen in the garden again. Then he was back on the dressing table, admiring himself in the mirror. Evidently, he had become enamoured of his own reflection. Grandfather observed that perhaps the attention he was receiving from everyone had made him a little conceited.

'He's trying to look better for Aunt Mabel,' I said, a remark that I instantly regretted, because Grandmother overheard it, and brought the flat of her broad hand down on my head.

'Well, now we know his weakness,' said Grandfather.

'Are you trying to be funny too?' demanded Grandmother, looking her most threatening.

'I only meant he was becoming very vain,' said Grandfather hastily. 'It should be easier to catch him now.'

He set about preparing a large cage with a mirror at one end. In the cage he left a juicy chicken and various other delicacies, and fitted up the opening with a trapdoor. Aunt Mabel had already left by the time we had this trap ready, but we had to go on with the project because we couldn't have the python prowling about the house indefinitely.

For a few days nothing happened, and then, as I was leaving for school one morning, I saw the python curled up in the cage. He had eaten everything left out for him, and was relaxing in front of the mirror with something resembling a smile on his face—if you can imagine a python smiling. I lowered the trapdoor gently, but the python took no notice; he was in raptures over his handsome reflection. Grandfather and the gardener put the cage in the ponytrap, and made a journey to the other side of the river bed. They left the cage in the jungle, with the trapdoor open.

'He made no attempt to get out,' said Grandfather later. 'And I didn't have the heart to take the mirror away. It's the first time I've seen a snake fall in love.'

The Elephant and the Cassowary Bird

THE BABY elephant, another of Grandfather's unusual pets, wasn't out of place in our home in north India because India is where elephants belong, and in any case our house was full of pets brought home by Grandfather, who was in the Forest Service. But the cassowary bird was different. No one had ever seen such a bird before—not in India, that is. Grandfather had picked it up on a voyage to Singapore, where he'd been given the bird by a rubber planter who'd got it from a Dutch trader who'd got it from a man in Indonesia.

Anyway, it ended up at our home in Dehra, and seemed to do quite well in the sub-tropical climate. It looked like a cross between a turkey and an ostrich, but bigger than the former and smaller than the latter—about five feet in height. It was not a beautiful bird, nor even a friendly one, but it had come to stay, and everyone was curious about it, especially the baby elephant.

Right from the start the baby elephant took a great interest in the cassowary. He would circle round the odd creature and diffidently examine with his trunk the texture of its stumpy wings; of course, he suspected no evil, and his childlike curiosity encouraged him to take liberties which resulted in an unpleasant experience.

Noticing the baby elephant's attempts to make friends with the rather morose cassowary, we felt a bit apprehensive. Self-contained and sullen, the big bird responded only by slowly and slyly raising one of its powerful legs, all the while gazing into space with an innocent air. We knew what the gesture meant: we had seen that treacherous leg raised on many an occasion, and suddenly shooting out with a force that would have done credit to a vicious camel. In fact, camel and cassowary kicks are delivered on the same plan, except that the camel kicks backward like a horse and the bird forward.

We wished to spare our baby elephant a painful experience, and led him away from the bird. But he persisted in his friendly overtures, and one morning he received an ugly reward. Rapid as lightning, the cassowary hit straight from the hip and knee joints and the elephant ran squealing to Grandfather.

For several days he avoided the cassowary, and we thought he had learnt his lesson. He crossed and recrossed the compound and the garden, swinging his trunk, thinking furiously. Then, a week later, he appeared on the veranda at breakfast time in his usual cheery, childlike fashion, sidling up to the cassowary as if nothing had happened.

We were struck with amazement at this and so, it seemed, was the bird. Had the painful lesson already been forgotten, that too by a member of the elephant tribe noted for its ability to never forget? Another dose of the same medicine would serve the booby right.

The cassowary once more began to draw up its fighting leg with sinister determination. It was nearing the true position for the master-kick, kung-fu style, when all of a sudden the baby elephant seized with his trunk the other leg of the cassowary and pulled it down. There was a clumsy flapping of wings, a tremendous swelling of the bird's wattle, and an undignified getting up, as if it were a floored boxer doing his best to beat the count of ten. The bird then marched off with an attempt to look stately and unconcerned, while we at the breakfast table were convulsed with laughter.

After this the cassowary bird gave the baby elephant as wide a berth as possible. But they were forced not to coexist for very long. The baby elephant, getting bulky and cumbersome, was sold to a zoo where he became a favourite with young visitors who loved to take rides on his back.

As for the cassowary, he continued to grace our veranda for many years, gaped at but not made much of, while entering on a rather friendless old age.

Monkey Trouble

GRANDFATHER BOUGHT Tutu from a street entertainer for a sum of ten rupees. The man had three monkeys. Tutu was the smallest but the most mischievous. She was tied up most of the time. The little monkey looked so miserable with a collar and chain that Grandfather decided it would be much happier in our home. Grandfather had a weakness for keeping unusual pets. It was a habit that I, at the age of eight or nine, used to encourage.

Grandmother at first objected to having a monkey in the house. 'You have enough pets as it is,' she said, referring to Grandfather's goat, several white mice, and a small tortoise.

'But I don't have any,' I said.

'You're wicked enough for two monkeys. One boy in the house is all I can take.'

'Ah, but Tutu isn't a boy,' said Grandfather triumphantly. 'This is a little girl monkey!'

Grandmother gave in. She had always wanted a little girl in the house. She believed girls were less troublesome than boys. Tutu was to prove her wrong.

She was a pretty little monkey. Her bright eyes sparkled with mischief beneath deep-set eyebrows. And her teeth, which were a pearly white, were often revealed in a grin that frightened the wits out of Aunt Ruby, whose nerves had already suffered from the presence of Grandfather's pet python in the house at Lucknow. But this was Dehra, my grandparents' house, and aunts and uncles had to put up with our pets.

Tutu's hands had a dried-up look, as though they had been pickled in the sun for many years. One of the first things I taught her was to shake hands, and this she insisted on doing with all who visited the house. Peppery Major Malik would have to stoop and shake hands with Tutu before he could enter the drawing room, otherwise Tutu would climb on his shoulder and stay there, roughing up his hair and playing with his moustache.

Uncle Benji couldn't stand any of our pets and took a particular dislike to Tutu, who was always making faces at him. But as Uncle Benji was never in a job for long, and depended on Grandfather's good-natured generosity, he had to shake hands with Tutu like everyone else.

Tutu's fingers were quick and wicked. And her tail, while adding to her good looks (Grandfather believed a tail would add to anyone's good looks!), also served as a third hand. She could use it to hang from a branch, and it was capable of scooping up any delicacy that might be out of reach of her hands.

Aunt Ruby had not been informed of Tutu's arrival. Loud shrieks from her bedroom brought us running to see what was wrong. It was only Tutu trying on Aunt Ruby's petticoats! They were much too large, of course, and when Aunt Ruby entered the room, all she saw was a faceless white blob jumping up and down on the bed.

We disentangled Tutu and soothed Aunt Ruby. I gave Tutu a bunch of sweet peas to make her happy. Granny didn't like anyone plucking her sweet peas, so I took some from Major Malik's garden while he was having his afternoon siesta.

Then Uncle Benji complained that his hairbrush was missing. We found Tutu sunning herself on the back veranda, using the hairbrush to scratch her armpits. I took it from her and handed it back to Uncle Benji with an apology; but he flung the brush away with an oath.

'Such a fuss about nothing,' I said. 'Tutu doesn't have fleas!'

'No, and she bathes more often than Benji,' said Grandfather, who had borrowed Aunt Ruby's shampoo for giving Tutu a bath.

All the same, Grandmother objected to Tutu being given the run of the house.

Tutu had to spend her nights in the outhouse, in the company of the goat. They got on quite well, and it was not long before Tutu was seen sitting comfortably on the back of the goat, while the goat roamed the back garden in search of its favourite grass.

The day Grandfather had to visit Meerut to collect his railway pension, he decided to take Tutu and me along—to keep us both out of mischief, he said. To prevent Tutu from wandering about on the train, causing inconvenience to passengers, she was provided with a large black travelling bag. This, with some straw at the bottom, became her compartment. Grandfather and I paid for our seats, and we took Tutu along as hand baggage.

There was enough space for Tutu to look out of the bag occasionally, and to be fed with bananas and biscuits, but she could not get her hands through the opening and the canvas was too strong for her to bite her way through.

Tutu's efforts to get out only had the effect of making the bag roll about on the floor or occasionally jump into the air—an exhibition that attracted a curious crowd of onlookers at the Dehra and Meerut railway stations.

Anyway, Tutu remained in the bag as far as Meerut, but while Grandfather was producing our tickets at the turnstile, she suddenly poked her head out of the bag and gave the ticket collector a wide grin.

The poor man was taken aback. But, with great presence of mind and much to Grandfather's annoyance, he said, 'Sir, you have a dog with you. You'll have to buy a ticket for it.'

'It is not a dog!' said Grandfather indignantly. 'This is a baby monkey of the species macacus-mischievous, closely related to the human species homus-horriblis! And there is no charge for babies!'

'It's as big as a cat,' said the ticket collector. 'Cats and dogs have to be paid for.'

'But I tell you it's only a baby!' protested Grandfather.

'Have you a birth certificate to prove that?' demanded the ticket collector.

'Next you'll be asking to see her mother,' snapped Grandfather.

In vain did he take Tutu out of the bag. In vain did he try to prove that a young monkey did not qualify as a dog or a cat or even as a quadruped. Tutu was classified as a dog by the ticket collector, and five rupees were handed over as her fare.

Then Grandfather, just to get his own back, took from his pocket the small tortoise that he sometimes carried about, and said: 'And what must I pay for this, since you charge for all creatures great and small?'

The ticket collector looked closely at the tortoise, prodded it with his forefinger, gave Grandfather a triumphant look, and said, 'No charge, sir. It is not a dog!'

Winters in north India can be very cold. A great treat for Tutu on winter evenings was the large bowl of hot water given to her by Grandmother for a bath. Tutu would cunningly test the temperature with her hand, then gradually step into the bath, first one foot, then the other (as she had seen me doing) until she was in the water up to her neck.

Once comfortable, she would take the soap in her hands or feet and rub herself all over. When the water became cold she would get out and run as quickly as she could to the kitchen fire in order to dry herself. If anyone laughed at her during this performance, Tutu's feelings would be hurt and she would refuse to go on with the bath.

One day Tutu almost succeeded in boiling herself alive. Grandmother had left a large kettle on the fire for tea. And Tutu, all by herself and with nothing better to do, decided to remove the lid. Finding the water just warm enough for a bath, she got in, with her head sticking out from the open kettle.

This was fine for a while, until the water began to get heated. Tutu raised herself a little. But finding it cold outside, she sat down again. She continued hopping up and down for some time until Grandmother returned and hauled her, half-boiled, out of the kettle.

'What's for tea today?' asked Uncle Benji gleefully. 'Boiled eggs and a half-boiled monkey?'

But Tutu was none the worse for the adventure and continued to bathe more regularly than Uncle Benji.

Aunt Ruby was a frequent taker of baths. This met with Tutu's approval—so much so, that one day, when Aunt Ruby had finished shampooing her hair she looked up through a lather of bubbles and soap-suds to see Tutu sitting opposite her in the bath, following her example.

One day Aunt Ruby took us all by surprise. She announced that she had become engaged. We had always thought Aunt Ruby would never marry—she had often said so herself—but it appeared that the right man had now come along in the person of Rocky Fernandes, a schoolteacher from Goa.

Rocky was a tall, firm-jawed, good-natured man, a couple of years younger than Aunt Ruby. He had a fine baritone voice and sang in the manner of the great Nelson Eddie. As Grandmother liked baritone singers, Rocky was soon in her good books.

'But what on earth does he see in her?' Uncle Benji wanted to know.

'More than any girl has seen in you!' snapped Grandmother. 'Ruby's a fine girl. And they're both teachers. Maybe they can start a school of their own.'

Rocky visited the house quite often and brought me chocolates and cashewnuts, of which he seemed to have an unlimited supply. He also taught me several marching songs. Naturally I approved of Rocky. Aunt Ruby won my grudging admiration for having made such a wise choice.

One day I overheard them talking of going to the bazaar to buy an engagement ring. I decided I would go along too. But as Aunt Ruby had made it clear that she did not want me around I decided that I had better follow at a discreet distance. Tutu, becoming aware that a mission of some importance was under way, decided to follow me. But as I had not invited her along, she too decided to keep out of sight.

Once in the crowded bazaar, I was able to get quite close to Aunt Ruby and Rocky without being spotted. I waited until they had settled down in a large jewellery shop before sauntering past and spotting them as though by accident. Aunt Ruby wasn't too pleased at seeing me, but Rocky waved and called out, 'Come and join us! Help your aunt choose a beautiful ring!'

The whole thing seemed to be a waste of good money, but I did not say so—Aunt Ruby was giving me one of her more unloving looks.

'Look, these are pretty!' I said, pointing to some cheap, bright agates set in white metal. But Aunt Ruby wasn't looking. She was immersed in a case of diamonds.

'Why not a ruby for Aunt Ruby?' I suggested, trying to please her.

'That's her lucky stone,' said Rocky. 'Diamonds are the thing for engagement.' And he started singing a song about a diamond being a girl's best friend.

While the jeweller and Aunt Ruby were sifting through the diamond rings, and Rocky was trying out another tune, Tutu had slipped into the shop without being noticed by anyone but me. A little squeal of delight was the first sign she gave of her presence. Everyone looked up to see her trying on a pretty necklace.

'And what are those stones?' I asked.

'They look like pearls,' said Rocky.

'They are pearls,' said the shopkeeper, making a grab for them.

'It's that dreadful monkey!' cried Aunt Ruby. 'I knew that boy would bring him here!'

The necklace was already adorning Tutu's neck. I thought she looked rather nice in them, but she gave us no time to admire the effect. Springing out of our reach Tutu dodged around Rocky, slipped between my legs, and made for the crowded road. I ran after her, shouting to her to stop, but she wasn't listening.

There were no branches to assist Tutu in her progress, but she used the heads and shoulders of people as springboards and so made rapid headway through the bazaar.

The jeweller left his shop and ran after us. So did Rocky. So did several bystanders who had seen the incident. And others, who had no idea what it was all about, joined in the chase. As Grandfather used to say, 'In a crowd, everyone plays follow-the-leader even when they don't know who's leading.' Not everyone knew that the leader was Tutu. Only the front runners could see her.

She tried to make her escape speedier by leaping on to the back of a passing scooterist. The scooter swerved into a fruit stall and came to a standstill under a heap of bananas, while the scooterist found himself in the arms of an indignant fruitseller. Tutu peeled a banana and ate part of it before deciding to move on.

From an awning she made an emergency landing on a washerman's donkey. The donkey promptly panicked and rushed down the road, while bundles of washing fell by the wayside. The washerman joined in the chase. Children on their way to school decided that here was something better to do than attend classes. With shouts of glee, they soon overtook their panting elders.

Tutu finally left the bazaar and took a road leading in the direction of our house. But knowing that she would be caught and locked up once she got home, she decided to end the chase by ridding herself of the necklace. Deftly removing it from her neck, she flung it in the small canal that ran down the road.

The jeweller, with a cry of anguish, plunged into the canal. So did Rocky. So did I. So did several other people, both adults and children. It was to be a treasure hunt!

Some twenty minutes later, Rocky shouted, 'I've found it!' Covered in mud, water-lilies, ferns and tadpoles, we emerged from the canal, and Rocky presented the necklace to the relieved shopkeeper.

Everyone trudged back to the bazaar to find Aunt Ruby waiting in the shop, still trying to make up her mind about a suitable engagement ring.

Finally the ring was bought, the engagement was announced, and a date was set for the wedding.

'I don't want that monkey anywhere near us on our wedding day,' declared Aunt Ruby.

'We'll lock her up in the outhouse,' promised Grandfather. 'And we'll let her out only after you've left for your honeymoon.'

A few days before the wedding I found Tutu in the kitchen helping Grandmother prepare the wedding cake. Tutu often helped with the cooking, and, when Grandmother wasn't looking, added herbs, spices, and other interesting items to the pots—so that occasionally we found a chilli in the custard or an onion in the jelly or a strawberry floating on the chicken soup.

Sometimes these additions improved a dish, sometimes they did not. Uncle Benji lost a tooth when he bit firmly into a sandwich which contained walnut shells.

I'm not sure exactly what went into that wedding cake when Grandmother wasn't looking—she insisted that Tutu was always very well-behaved in the kitchen—but I did spot Tutu stirring in some red chilli sauce, bitter gourd seeds, and a generous helping of eggshells!

It's true that some of the guests were not seen for several days after the wedding but no one said anything against the cake. Most people thought it had an interesting flavour.

The great day dawned, and the wedding guests made their way to the little church that stood on the outskirts of Dehra—a town with a church, two mosques, and several temples.

I had offered to dress Tutu up as a bridesmaid and bring her along, but no one except Grandfather thought it was a good idea. So I was an obedient boy and locked Tutu in the outhouse. I did, however, leave the skylight open a little. Grandmother had always said that fresh air was good for growing children, and I thought Tutu should have her share of it.

The wedding ceremony went without a hitch. Aunt Ruby looked a picture, and Rocky looked like a film star.

Grandfather played the organ, and did so with such gusto that the small choir could hardly be heard. Grandmother cried a little, I sat quietly in a corner, with the little tortoise on my lap.

When the service was over, we trooped out into the sunshine and made our way back to the house for the reception.

The feast had been laid out on tables in the garden. As the gardener had been left in charge, everything was in order. Tutu was on her best behaviour. She had, it appeared, used the skylight to avail of more fresh air outside, and now sat beside the three-tier wedding cake, guarding it against crows, squirrels and the goat. She greeted the guests with squeals of delight.

It was too much for Aunt Ruby. She flew at Tutu in a rage. And Tutu, sensing that she was not welcome, leapt away, taking with her the top tier of the wedding cake.

Led by Major Malik, we followed her into the orchard, only to find that she had climbed to the top of the jackfruit tree. From there she proceeded to pelt us with bits of wedding cake. She had also managed to get hold of a bag of confetti, and when she ran out of cake she showered us with confetti.

'That's more like it!' said the good-humoured Rocky. 'Now let's return to the party, folks!'

Uncle Benji remained with Major Malik, determined to chase Tutu away. He kept throwing stones into the tree, until he received a large piece of cake bang on his nose. Muttering threats, he returned to the party, leaving the Major to do battle.

When the festivities were finally over, Uncle Benji took out the old car out of the garage and drove up to the veranda steps. He was going to drive Aunt Ruby and Rocky to the nearby hill-resort of Mussoorie, where they would have their honeymoon.

Watched by family and friends, Aunt Ruby and Rocky climbed into the back seat. Aunt Ruby waved regally to everyone. She leant out of the window and offered me her cheek and I had to kiss her farewell. Everyone wished them luck.

As Rocky burst into song Uncle Benji opened the throttle and stepped on the accelerator. The car shot forward in a cloud of dust.

Rocky and Aunt Ruby continued to wave to us. And so did Tutu from her perch on the rear bumper! She was clutching a bag in her hands and showering confetti on all who stood in the driveway.

'They don't know Tutu's with them!' I exclaimed. 'She'll go all the way to Mussoorie! Will Aunt Ruby let her stay with them?'

'Tutu might ruin the honeymoon,' said Grandfather. 'But don't worry—Benji will bring her back!'

Harold, Our Hornbill

HAROLD'S MOTHER, like all good hornbills, was the most careful of wives. His father was the most easy-going of husbands. In January, long before the flame tree flowered, Harold's father took his wife into a great hole high in the tree trunk, where his father and his father's father had taken their brides at the same time every year.

In this weather-beaten hollow, generation upon generation of hornbills had been raised. Harold's mother, like those before her, was enclosed within the hole by a sturdy wall of earth, sticks and dung.

Harold's father left a small hole in the centre of this wall to enable him to communicate with his wife whenever he felt like a chat. Walled up in her uncomfortable room, Harold's mother was a prisoner for over two months. During this period an egg was laid, and Harold was born.

In his naked boyhood Harold was no beauty. His most promising feature was his flaming red bill, matching the blossoms of the flame tree which was now ablaze, heralding the summer. He had a stomach that could never be filled, despite the best efforts of his parents who brought him pieces of jackfruit and berries from the banyan tree.

As he grew bigger, the room became more cramped, and one day his mother burst through the wall, spread out her wings and sailed over the tree-tops. Her husband was glad to see her about. He played with her, expressing his delight with deep gurgles and throaty chuckles. Then they repaired the wall of the nursery, so that Harold would not fall out.

Harold was quite happy in his cell, and felt no urge for freedom. He was putting on weight and a philosophy of his own. Then something happened to change the course of his life.

One afternoon he was awakened from his siesta by a loud thumping on the wall, a sound quite different from that made by his parents. Soon the wall gave way, and there was something large and yellow and furry staring at him—not his parents' bills, but the hungry eyes of a civet cat.

Before Harold could be seized, his parents flew at the cat, both roaring lustily and striking out with their great bills. In the ensuing melee, Harold tumbled out of his nest and landed on our garden path.

Before the cat or any predator could get to him, Grandfather picked him up and took him to the sanctuary of the veranda.

Harold had lost some wing feathers and did not look as though he would be able to survive on his own, so we made an enclosure for him on our front veranda. Grandfather and I took over the duties of his parents.

Harold had a simple outlook, and once he had got over some early attacks of nerves, he began to welcome the approach of people. Grandfather and I meant the arrival of food and he greeted us with craning neck, quivering open bill and a loud, croaking, 'Ka-ka-kaee!'

Fruit, insect or animal food, and green leaves were all welcome. We soon dispensed with the enclosure, but Harold made no effort to go away; he had difficulty flying. In fact, he asserted his tenancy rights, at least as far as the veranda was concerned.

One afternoon a veranda tea party was suddenly and alarmingly convulsed by a flash of black and white and noisy flapping. And behold, the last and only loaf of bread had been seized and carried off to his perch near the ceiling.

Harold was not beautiful by Hollywood standards. He had a small body and a large head. But he was good-natured and friendly, and he remained on good terms with most members of the household during his lifetime of 12 years.

Harold's best friends were those who fed him, and he was willing even to share his food with us, sometimes trying to feed me with his great beak.

While I turned down his offers of beetles and similar delicacies, I did occasionally share a banana with him. Eating was a serious business for Harold, and if there was any delay at mealtimes he would summon me with raucous barks and vigorous bangs of his bill on the woodwork of the kitchen window.

Having no family, profession or religion, Harold gave much time and thought to his personal appearance. He carried a rouge pot on his person and used it very skillfully as an item of his morning toilet.

This rouge pot was a small gland situated above the roots of his tail feathers;

it produced a rich yellow fluid. Harold would dip into his rouge pot from time to time and then rub the colour over his feathers and the back of his neck. It would come off on my hands whenever I touched him.

Harold would toy with anything bright or glittering, often swallowing it afterwards.

He loved bananas and dates and balls of boiled rice. I would throw him the rice balls, and he would catch them in his beak, toss them in the air, and let them drop into his open mouth.

He perfected this trick of catching things, and in time I taught him to catch a tennis ball thrown with some force from a distance of 15 yards. He would have made a great baseball catcher or an excellent slip fielder. On one occasion he seized a rupee coin from me (a week's pocket money in those days) and swallowed it neatly.

Only once did he really misbehave. That was when he removed a lighted cigar from the hand of an American cousin who was visiting us. Harold swallowed the cigar. It was a moving experience for Harold, and an unnerving one for our guest.

Although Harold never seemed to drink any water, he loved the rain. We always knew when it was going to rain because Harold would start chuckling to himself about an hour before the first raindrops fell.

This used to irritate Aunt Ruby. She was always being caught in the rain. Harold would be chuckling when she left the house. And when she returned, drenched to the skin, he would be in fits of laughter.

As storm clouds would gather, and gusts of wind would shake the banana trees, Harold would get very excited, and his chuckle would change to an eerie whistle.

'Wheee...wheee,' he would scream, and then, as the first drops of rain hit the veranda steps, and the scent of the fresh earth passed through the house, he would start roaring with pleasure.

The wind would carry the rain into the veranda, and Harold would spread out his wings and dance, tumbling about like a circus clown. My grandparents and I would come out on the veranda and share his happiness.

Many years later, I still miss Harold's raucous bark and the banging of his great bill. If there is a heaven for good hornbills, I sincerely hope he is getting all the summer showers he could wish for, and plenty of tennis balls to catch.

Owls in the Family

ONE MORNING we found a full-fledged baby spotted owlet on the ground by the veranda steps. When Grandfather picked it up, it hissed and clacked its bill, but, after a meal of raw meat and water, settled down for the day under my bed.

The spotted owlet, even when full grown, is only the size of a myna, and has none of the sinister appearance of the larger owls. A pair of them may often be found in an old mango or tamarind tree, and by tapping on the tree trunk you may be able to persuade the bird to show an enquiring face at the entrance to its hole. The bird is not normally afraid of man, nor is it strictly a night-bird; but it prefers to stay at home during the day, as it is sometimes attacked by other birds, who consider all owls as their enemies.

The little owlet was quite happy under my bed. The following day a second owlet was found in almost the same place on the veranda, and only then did we realize that where the rainwater pipe emerged through the roof, there was a rough sort of nest, from which the birds had fallen. We took the second young owl to join the first, and fed them both. When I went to bed they were on the ledge just inside the mosquito netting, and later in the night their mother found them there. From outside she crooned and gurgled for a long time, and in the morning I found that she had left a mouse with its tail tucked through the mosquito net! Obviously she placed no reliance on me as a foster-parent.

The young birds throve and, ten days later at dawn, Grandfather and I took them into the garden to release them. I had placed one on a branch of the mango tree, and was stooping to pick up the other, when I received quite a heavy blow on the back of my head. A second or two later, the mother owl swooped down at Grandfather, but he was agile enough to duck out of its way. Quickly I placed the second owl under the mango tree. Then from a safe distance we watched the mother fly down and lead her offspring into the long grass at the edge of the garden.

We thought she would take her family away from the vicinity of our rather strange household; but next morning, on coming out of my room, I found two young owls standing on the wall just outside the door! I ran to tell Grandfather, and when we came back we found the mother sitting on the bird-bath 10 yards away. She was evidently feeling sorry for her behaviour the previous day, because she greeted us with a soft 'whoo-whoo'.

'Now there's an unselfish mother for you!' said Grandfather. 'It's obvious she'd like them to have a good home. And they're probably getting a bit too big for her to manage.'

So the two owlets became regular members of our household, and, strangely enough, were among the few pets that Grandmother took a liking to. She objected to all snakes, most monkeys, and some crows,

but she took quite a fancy to the owls, and frequently fed them on spaghetti. They seemed quite fond of spaghetti. In fact, the owls became so attached to Grandmother that they began to show affection towards anyone in a petticoat, including Aunt Mabel, who was terrified of them. She would run shrieking from the room every time one of the birds sidled up to her in a friendly manner.

Forgetful of the fact that Grandfather and I had reared them, the owls would sometimes swell their feathers and snap at anyone in trousers. To avoid displeasing them, Grandfather wore a petticoat at feeding time. This mild form of transvestism appeared to satisfy them. I compromised by wearing an apron.

In response to Grandmother's voice, the owlets would make sounds as gentle and soothing as the purring of a cat; but when wild owls were around, ours would rend the night with blood-curdling shrieks. Their nightly occupation was catching beetles, with which the kitchen-quarters were infested at the time. With their sharp eyes and powerful beaks they were excellent pest destroyers.

The owls loved to sit and splash in a shallow dish, especially if cold water was poured over them from a jug at the same time. They would get thoroughly wet, jump out on to a perch, shake themselves, then return for a second splash and sometimes a third. During the day they dozed in large cages under the trees in the garden. They needed cages for protection against attacks from wild birds. At night they had the freedom of the house, where they exercised their wings as much as they liked. Superstitious folk, who dread the cry of the owl, may be interested to know that—mice excepted—there were no untoward deaths in the house during the owls' residence.

Looking back on those owlish days, I carry in my mind a picture of Grandmother with a contented look in her rocking-chair. Once, on entering her room while she was having an afternoon nap, I saw that one of the owls had crawled up her pillow till its head was snuggled under her ear. Both Grandmother and the little owl were snoring.

Uncle Ken's Rumble in the Jungle

UNCLE KEN drove Grandfather's old Fiat along the forest road at an incredible 30 mph, scattering pheasants, partridges and jungle fowl as he clattered along. He had come in search of the disappearing red jungle fowl, and I could see why the bird had disappeared. Too many noisy human beings had invaded its habitat.

By the time we reached the forest rest house, one of the car doors had fallen off its hinges, and a large lantana bush had got entwined in the bumper.

'Never mind,' said Uncle Ken. 'It's all part of the adventure!'

The rest house had been reserved for Uncle Ken, thanks to Grandfather's good relations with the forest department. But I was the only other person in the car. No one else would trust himself or herself to Uncle Ken's driving. He treated a car as though it were a low-flying aircraft having some difficulty in getting off the runway.

As we arrived at the rest house, a number of hens made a dash for safety.

'Look jungle fowl!' exclaimed Uncle Ken.

'Domestic fowl,' I said. 'They must belong to the forest guards.'

I was right, of course. One of the hens was destined to be served up as chicken curry later that day. The jungle birds avoided the neighbourhood of the rest house, just in case they were mistaken for poultry and went into the cooking pot.

Uncle Ken was all for starting his search right away, and after a brief interval during which we were served tea with pakoras (prepared by the forest guard, who it turned out was also a good cook) we set off on foot into the jungle in search of the elusive red jungle fowl.

'No tigers on this range,' said the guard. 'Just elephants.'

Uncle Ken wasn't afraid of elephants. He'd been for numerous elephant rides at the Lucknow zoo. He'd also seen Sabu in *Elephant Boy*.

A small wooden bridge took us across a little river, and then we were in thick jungle, following the forest guard who led us along a path that was frequently blocked by broken tree branches and pieces of bamboo.

'Why all these broken branches?' asked Uncle Ken.

'The elephants, sir,' replied our guard. 'They passed through last night. They like certain leaves, as well as young bamboo shoots.'

We saw a number of spotted deer and several pheasants, but no red jungle fowl. That evening we sat out on the veranda of the rest house. All was silent, except for the distant trumpeting of elephants. Then, from the stream, came the chanting of hundreds of frogs.

There were tenors and baritones, sopranos and contraltos, and occasionally a bass deep enough to have pleased the great Chaliapin. They sang duets and quartets from *La Boheme* and other Italian operas, drowning out all other jungle sounds except for the occasional cry of a jackal doing his best to join in.

'We might as well sing,' said Uncle Ken, and began singing the 'Indian love call' in his best Nelson Eddy manner.

The frogs fell silent, obviously awestruck; but instead of receiving an answering love call, Uncle Ken was answered by even more strident jackal calls—not one, but several—with the result that all self-respecting denizens of the forest fled from the vicinity, and we saw no wildlife that night apart from a frightened rabbit that sped across the clearing and vanished into the darkness.

Early next morning we renewed our efforts to track down the red jungle fowl, but it remained elusive. Returning to the rest house dusty and weary, Uncle Ken exclaimed: 'There it is—a red jungle fowl!'

But it turned out to be the caretaker's cock-bird, a handsome fellow all red and gold, but not the jungle variety.

Disappointed, Uncle Ken decided to return to civilization. Another night in the rest house did not appeal to him. He had run out of songs to sing.

In any case, the weather had changed overnight and a light drizzle was falling as we started out. This had turned into a steady downpour by the time we reached the bridge across the Suswa river. And standing in the middle of the bridge was an elephant.

He was a lone tusker and didn't look too friendly.

Uncle Ken blew his horn, and that was a mistake.

It was a strident, penetrating horn, highly effective on city roads but out of place in the forest. The elephant took it as a challenge, and returned the blast of the horn with a shrill trumpeting of its own. It took a few steps forward. Uncle Ken put the car into reverse.

'Is there another way out of here?' he asked.

'There's a side road,' I said recalling an earlier trip with Grandfather. 'It will take us to the Kansrao railway station.'

'What ho!' cried Uncle Ken. 'To the station we go!'

And he turned the car and drove back until we came to the turning.

The narrow road was now a rushing torrent of rainwater and all Uncle Ken's driving skills were put to the test. He had on one occasion driven through a brick wall, so he knew all about obstacles; but they were normally stationary ones.

'More elephants,' I said, as two large pachyderms loomed out of the rain-drenched forest.

'Elephants to the right of us, elephants to the left of us!' chanted Uncle Ken, misquoting Tennyson's 'Charge of the Light Brigade'. 'Into the valley of death rode six hundred!'

'There are now three of them,' I observed.

'Not my lucky number,' said Uncle Ken and pressed hard on the accelerator. We lurched forward, almost running over a terrified barking deer.

'Is four your lucky number, Uncle Ken?'

'Why do you ask?'

'Well, there are now four of them behind us. And they are catching up quite fast!'

'I see the station ahead,' cried Uncle Ken, as we drove into a clearing where a tiny railway station stood like a beacon of safety in the wilderness.

The car came to a grinding halt. We abandoned it and ran for the building.

The stationmaster saw our predicament and beckoned to us to enter the station building, which was little more than a two-room shed and platform. He took us inside his tiny control room and shut the steel gate behind us.

'The elephants won't bother you here,' he said. 'But say goodbye to your car.'

We looked out of the window and were horrified to see Grandfather's Fiat overturned by one of the elephants, while another proceeded to trample it underfoot. The other elephants joined in the mayhem and soon the car was a flattened piece of junk.

'I'm Stationmaster Abdul Rauf,' the friendly stationmaster introduced himself. 'I know a good scrap dealer in Doiwala. I'll give you his address.'

'But how do we get out of here?' asked Uncle Ken.

'Well, it's only an hour's walk to Doiwala,' said our benefactor. 'But I wouldn't advise walking, not with those elephants around. Stay and have a cup of tea. The Dehra Express will pass through shortly. It stops for a few minutes. And it's only half an hour to Dehra from here.'

He punched out a couple of rail tickets. 'Here you are, my friends. Just two rupees each. The cheapest rail journey in India. And those tickets carry an insurance value of two lakh rupees each, should an accident befall you between here and Dehradun.'

Uncle Ken's eyes lit up. 'You mean, if one of us falls out of the train?' he asked.

'Out of the moving train,' clarified the stationmaster. 'There will be an enquiry, of course. Some people try to fake an accident.'

But Uncle Ken decided against falling out of the train and making a fortune. He'd had enough excitement for the day. We got home safely enough, taking a pony-cart from the Dehra station to our house.

'Where's my car?' asked Grandfather, as we staggered up the veranda steps.

'It had a small accident,' said Uncle Ken. 'We left it outside the Kansrao railway station. I'll collect it later.'

'I'm starving,' I said. 'Haven't eaten since morning.'

'Well, come and have your dinner,' said Granny. 'I've made something special for you. One of your Grandfather's hunting friends sent us a jungle fowl. I've made a nice roast. Try it with apple sauce.'

Uncle Ken did not ask if the jungle fowl was red, grey or technicoloured. He was first to the dining table.

Granny had anticipated this, and served me with a chicken leg, giving the other leg to Grandfather.

'I rather fancy the breast myself,' she said, and this left Uncle Ken with a long and scrawny neck—which was rather like his own neck, and more than he deserved.

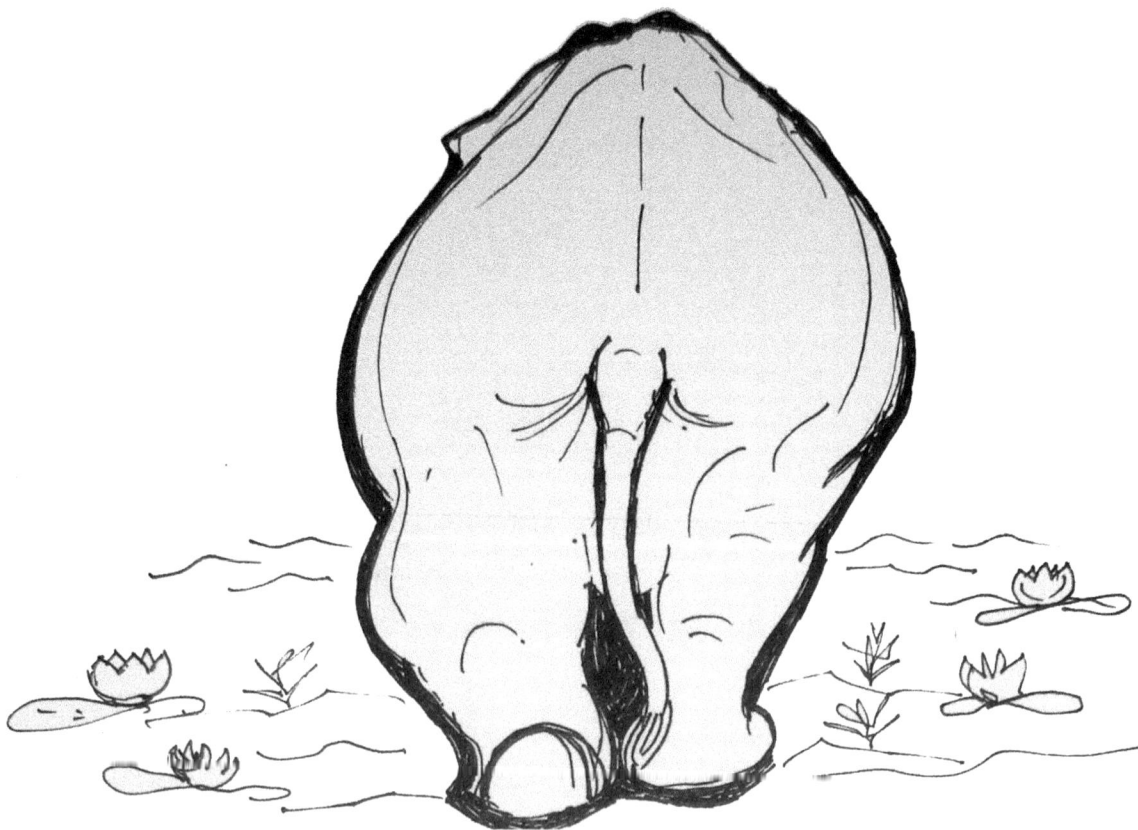

A Wilderness in Delhi

IF YOU are determined, you can find a wilderness close to you, no matter where you live. In 1959, I was living on the outskirts of a greater, further New Delhi. The influx of refugees from the Punjab after Partition had led to many new colonies springing up on the outskirts of the capital, and at the time the furthest of these was Rajouri Garden. Needless to say, there were no gardens. The treeless colony was buffeted by hot, dusty winds from Haryana and Rajasthan. The houses were built on one side of Najafgarh Road. On the other side, as yet uncolonized, were extensive fields of wheat and other crops still belonging to the original inhabitants. In an attempt to escape the city life that constantly oppressed me, I would walk across the main road and into the fields, finding old wells, irrigation channels, camels and buffaloes, and sighting birds and small creatures that no longer dwelt in the city life that led to my taking a greater interest in the natural world. Up to that time, I had taken it all for granted.

The notebook I kept at the time lies before me now, and my first entry describes the blue jays or rollers that were much a feature of those remaining open spaces. At rest, the bird is fairly nondescript but when it takes flight it reveals the glorious bright blue wings and the tail, banded with a lighter blue. It sits motionless, but the large dark eyes are constantly watching the ground in every direction. A grasshopper or cricket has only to make a brief appearance, and the blue jay will launch itself straight at its prey. In spring and early summer the 'roller' lives up to its other name. It indulges in love flights in which it rises and falls in the air with harsh grating screams—a real rock and roller!

Some way down the Najafgarh Road was a large village pond and beside it a magnificent banyan tree. We have no place for banyan trees today, they need so much space in which to spread their limbs and live comfortably. Cut away its aerial roots and the great tree topples over—usually to make way for a spacious apartment building. That was the first banyan tree I got to know well. It had about a hundred pillars supporting the boughs, and above them there was this great leafy crown like a pillared hall. It has been said that whole armies could shelter in the shade of an old banyan. And probably at one time they did. I saw another sort of army visit the banyan by the village pond when it was in fruit. Parakeets, mynas, rosy pastors, crested bulbuls without crests, barbets and many other birds crowded the tree in order to feast noisily on big, scarlet figs.

Even further down the Najafgarh Road was a large jheel, famous for its fishing. I wonder if any part of the jheel still exists, or if it got filled in and became a part of greater Delhi. One could rest in the shade of a small babul or keekar tree and watch the kingfisher skim over the water, making just a slight splash as it dived and came up with small glistening fish. Our common Indian kingfisher is a beautiful little bird with a brilliant blue back, a white throat and orange underparts. I would spot one perched on an overhanging bush or rock, and wait to see

it plunge like an arrow into the water and return to its perch to devour the catch. It came over the water in a flash of gleaming blue, shrilling its loud 'tit-tit-tit'.

The kingfisher is the subject of a number of legends, and the one I remember best, recounted by Romain Rolland, tells us that it was originally a plain grey bird that acquired its resplendent colours by flying straight towards the sun when Noah let it out of the Ark. Its upper plumage took the colour of the sky above, while the lower was scorched a deep russet by the rays of the setting sun.

Summer and winter, I scorned the dust and the traffic, and walked all over Delhi, in search of quiet spots with some shade, a few birds, flower and fruit. I spent many afternoons lying on the grass near India Gate and eating jamuns. I still remember the sour tang of the jamun which was best eaten with a little salt.

After I settled down in Mussoorie, I would visit Delhi very often, and I came to the heretical conclusion that there is more bird life in the cities than there is in the woods and forests around our hill stations.

For birds to survive, they must learn to live with and off humans; and those birds, like crows, sparrows and mynas, who do this to perfection, continue to thrive as our cities grow; whereas the purely wild birds, those who depend upon the forests for life, are rapidly disappearing, simply because the forests are disappearing.

On a recent visit, I saw more birds in one week in a New Delhi colony than I had seen during a month in the hills. Here, one must be patient and alert if one is to spot just a few of the birds so beautifully described in Salim Ali's *Indian Hill Birds*. The babblers and thrushes are still around, but the flycatchers and warblers are seldom seen or heard.

In a city like Delhi, however, if you have just a bit of garden and perhaps a guava tree, you will be visited by bulbuls, tailorbirds, mynas, hoopoes, parrots and tree pies. Or, if you own an old house, you will have to share it with pigeons and, perhaps, swallows or swifts (the sparrows, sadly, have abandoned the city). And if you have neither garden nor rooftop, you will still be visited by the crows.

Where the man goes, the crow follows. He has learnt to perfection the art of living off humans. He will, I am sure, be the first bird on the moon, scavenging among the paper bags and cartons left behind by untidy astronauts.

Crows favour the densest areas of human population, and there must be at least one for every human. Many crows seem to have been humans in their previous lives; they possess

all the cunning and sense of self-preservation of man. At the same time, there are many humans who have obviously been crows; we haven't lost our thieving instincts.

Watch a crow sidling along the garden wall with a shabby, genteel air, cocking a speculative eye at the kitchen door and any attendant humans. He reminds one of a newspaper reporter, hovering in the background until his chance comes— and then pouncing! I have even known a crow to make off with an egg from the breakfast table. No other bird, except perhaps the sparrow, has been so successful in exploiting human beings.

The myna, although he too is quite at home in the city, is more of a gentleman. He prefers fruit on the tree to scraps from the kitchen, and visits the garden as much out of a sense of sociability as in expectation of handouts. He is quite handsome, too, with his bright orange bill and the mask around his eyes. He is equally at home on a railway platform as on the ear of a grazing buffalo, and, being omnivorous, has no trouble in coexisting with man.

Although the blue jay, or roller, is quite capable of making his living in the forest, he also seems to show a preference for the haunts of men, and would rather perch on a telegraph wire than in a tree. Probably he finds the wire a better launching pad for his sudden rocket-flights and aerial acrobatics.

In repose he is rather shabby; but in flight, when his outspread wings reveal his brilliant blues, he takes one's breath away. As his food consists of beetles and other insect pests, he can be considered man's friend and ally.

Parrots make little or no distinction between town and country life. They are the freelancers of the bird world—sturdy, independent and noisy. With flashes of blue and green, they swoop across the road, settle for a while in a mango tree, and then, with shrill, delighted cries, move on to some other field or orchard.

They will sample all the fruit they can, without finishing any. They are

destructive birds but, because of their bright plumage, graceful flight and charming ways, they are popular favourites and can get away with anything. No one who has enjoyed watching a flock of parrots in swift and carefeee flight could want to cage one of these virile birds. Yet so many people do cage them.

After the peacock, perhaps the most popular bird in rural India is the sarus crane—a familiar sight around the jheels and river-banks of northern India and Gujarat. The sarus pairs for life and is seldom seen without his mate. When one bird dies, the other often pines away and seemingly dies of grief. It is this near-human quality of devotion that has earned the bird their popularity with the villagers of the plains. As a result, they are well protected.

In the long run, it is the 'common man', and not the scientist or conservationist, who can best give protection to the birds and animals living around him. Religious sentiment has helped preserve the peacock, the sarus. It is a pity that so many other equally beautiful birds do not enjoy the same protection.

A Year with Suzie

SUZIE CAME into my life when she was just three weeks old—really too small a baby to be adopted by an inexperienced bachelor. Perhaps I should make it clear at the start that Suzie is a Siamese cat.

I had told a friend that I needed a pet to share my rather lonely life on the outskirts of Mussoorie, which I had decided to make my home when I was 30. I had expected to receive a dog; but when the kitten arrived, its small questing head with the chocolate-tipped ears thrust out of a friend's coat pocket, I fell in love at first sight. And, taking its sex for granted, I named the kitten Suzie.

Suzie spent her first night curled up in a tea cosy. She showed her good breeding right from the start by selecting a commodious pot of geraniums for her morning ablutions. A puppy, I reflected, would have been less discriminating.

Like most Siamese cats, she showed a dislike for milk; and I was faced with the problem of obtaining a regular supply of meat. As I lived two miles from the nearest butcher, I took meat only once or twice a week; but Suzie disdained a vegetarian diet. I solved the problem by purchasing a month's supply of tinned sardines and feeding her exclusively on fish. She liked butter too, and used it to polish her coat. All this proved expensive, but I was hoping that as she grew older her natural instincts would result in her bringing in her own supplies.

I was not disappointed. She was barely a month old when she snapped up a large moth that flew in through the open windows on a balmy September night.

With all the savage artistry of her species, Suzie dissected this choice morsel and devoured it with relish. A few days later I found, on the kitchen floor, the head and tail of a mouse. The bright innocence of Suzie's sky blue eyes told me where the rest of the mouse was now lodged.

Cats rarely answer to their names; but Suzie often does. Moreover, I had tied a little bell to her neck, and this generally tells me where she is. Her favourite haunt is a cherry tree. When a pair of thrushes were building a nest, Suzie learnt to climb this tree beautifully—and the birds went elsewhere. There is truth in the saying that the cat is the aunt of the tiger, and taught the tiger everything except how to climb a tree.

If a cat and a dog are properly introduced to each other, they make the best of friends. It did not take Suzie long to develop a playful, nose-tapping relationship with my neighbour's dog, Peke. Another dog, a rather doleful, good-natured Cocker, permitted Suzie to sleep beneath her on cold days. Such was Suzie's charm that she was soon being fed by my neighbours, and this generosity solved my food problems. People took pity on us. Bachelors and kittens are suitable objects for compassion.

Suzie must have been about five months old when I discovered, to my dismay and embarrassment, that my cat was really a male. But I scorned all suggestions for a change of name: he had been Suzie from his infancy, and he would keep his girl's name for the rest of his time with me.

I had been warned that as soon as Suzie was eight months old he would start staying out late at nights, or even remaining away for several days in his search for a suitable mate. But Suzie was not like other males. He stayed at home, and the queens came to him. There was a beautiful black creature with yellow eyes, straight out of Edgar Allan Poe, and a handsome wild cat from the forest, who came to the front door on alternate nights (never together). Suzie would go out and meet his admirers, and frolic with them in the long, dew-drenched monsoon grass, before returning indoors to sleep deeply and sweetly at the foot of my bed.

Suzie likes people. I think he finds them comfortable. If there are guests, he will always choose the one with the broadest, most accommodating lap. At night he usually sleeps on my tummy (he likes its rise and fall, as I breathe) and if it gets cold, he curls up in the hollow behind my knees.

In the house, during the day, he is unobtrusive. Outside, he has his own pursuits and pleasures, whether it be stalking garden lizards or too familiar mynas and crows. Sometimes I find him curled up on my typewriter, reminding me that I have not been working regularly of late. He likes music (or is it just the vibrations from the set?) and a favourite spot of his, ever since childhood, has been beside the radio.

At the time of writing Suzie is in the garden, among the marigolds. I doubt if he will find any lizards there. But perhaps this time he is only looking for fairies.

My Three Bears

MOST HIMALAYAN villages lie in the valleys, where there are small streams, fairly fertile soil, and protection from the biting winds that come through the mountain passes in winter. The houses are usually made of rough granite, and have sloping slate roofs so that the heavy monsoon rain can slide off easily. During the dry autumn months, the roofs are often covered with pumpkins, left there to ripen in the sun.

One October night, when I was sleeping in a friend's house in a village up in the mountains, I was woken up by a thumping on the roof. I woke my friend and asked him what was happening.

'It's only a bear,' he said.

'Is it trying to get in?' I asked.

'No, it's after the pumpkins.'

And a little later, when we looked out of the small window, we saw a black bear making off through a field like a thief in the night, a pumpkin held to his chest. That was the first bear I had seen in the wild.

In winter, when snow covers the higher mountains, the brown and black Himalayan bears descend to lower altitudes in search of food. Sometimes, they forage in fields. Because they are short-sighted and suspicious of anything that moves, they can be dangerous; but, like most wild animals, they will avoid

human beings if they can, and are aggressive only when accompanied by their cubs.

The people of the hills always advise me to run downhill if chased by a bear. They say that bears find it easier to run uphill than downhill! I have yet to be chased by a bear, but I have seen three; and two of these encounters were quite comical.

Once, while I was sitting in a spruce tree, hoping to see a pair of pine martens that lived nearby, I heard the whining grumble of a bear, and presently a small bear ambled into the clearing beneath the tree.

He was little more than a cub, and I was not alarmed. I sat very still, waiting to see what he would do.

At first he put his nose to the ground and sniffed his way along until he came to a large anthill. Here he began huffing and puffing, blowing rapidly in and out of his nostrils, so that the dust from the anthill flew in all directions. But he was a disappointed bear, because the anthill had long since been deserted. And so, grumbling, he made his way to a wild plum tree, and shinning rapidly up the smooth trunk, was soon settled on the topmost branches. It was only then that he saw me.

The bear at once scrambled several feet higher up the tree and laid himself out flat on a branch. As it wasn't a thick branch, it left a large expanse of the bear showing on either side. He tucked his head away behind another branch, and so long as he could not see me, was well satisfied that he was completely hidden, although he couldn't help grumbling with anxiety.

But, like all bears, he was full of curiosity. And slowly, inch by inch, his black snout appeared over the edge of the branch.

As soon as his eyes met mine, he drew his head back with a jerk and hid his face.

The young bear did this several times. I waited until he wasn't looking, then moved some way down the tree. When the bear looked up again and saw that I was missing, he was so pleased that he stretched right across to another branch and helped himself to a plum. At that, I couldn't help bursting into laughter.

The startled young bear tumbled out of the tree, dropped through the branches for some 15 feet, and landed with a thud on a heap of dry leaves. He was quite unhurt, but ran from the clearing, grunting and squealing with fright. So much for my second bear.

My third bear also revealed the inquisitiveness of the species.

I was staying with another friend, Prem, in his village in Garhwal, when we learnt that an adult bear had been active in a field of maize. We took up our position on a high outcrop of rock, which gave us a clear view of the moonlit field.

A little after midnight, a big bear came down to the edge of the field, but he was suspicious and probably smelt that men were in the vicinity. But he was hungry. And so, after standing up as high as possible on his hind legs and peering about to see whether or not the field was empty, he came cautiously into the open and made his way towards the maize.

When about half-way, however, his attention was suddenly attracted by some Tibetan prayer flags which had been strung up between two trees. On spotting the flags, the bear gave a little grunt of disapproval and began backing away. But the fluttering of the little flags was a puzzle that he felt he had to figure out; and so, after a few backward steps, he again stopped and watched them.

Now he advanced until he was within a few yards of the flags. Then he again got on his hind legs and examined them from different angles. Seeing that they did not attack him or appear in any way dangerous, he made his way right up to the flags, taking only two or three steps at a time, and having a good look each time before advancing. Eventually he went confidently up to the flags and pulled them all down. Then, after examining them carefully, he moved into the field of maize.

But my friend, Prem, to whom the field belonged, decided that he wasn't going to lose any more maize. So he started shouting and the villagers woke up and came out of their houses beating drums and empty kerosene tins.

Deprived of his dinner, the bear made off in a bad temper. He ran downhill, and at a good speed too, and I am glad I wasn't in his path just then. Uphill or downhill, an angry bear is best given a very wide berth.

A New Flower

IT WAS the first day of spring (according to the Hindu calendar), but here in the Himalayas it still seemed midwinter. A cold wind hummed and whistled through the pines, while dark rain-clouds were swept along by the west wind only to be thrust back by the east wind.

I was climbing the steep road to my cottage at the top of the hill when I was overtaken by nine-year-old Usha hurrying back from school. She had tied a scarf round her head to keep her hair from blowing about. Dark hair and eyes, and pink cheeks, were all accentuated by the patches of snow still lying on the hillside.

'Look,' she said, pointing. 'A new flower!' It was a single, butter-yellow blossom, and it stood out like a bright star against the drab winter grass. I hadn't seen anything like it before, and had no idea what its name might be. No doubt its existence was recorded in some botanical tome. But for me it was a discovery.

'Shall I pick it for you?' asked Usha. 'No, don't,' I said. 'It may be the only one. If we break it, there may not be any more. Let's leave it there and see if it seeds.' We scrambled up the slope and examined the flower more closely. It was very delicate and soft-petalled, looking as though it might fall at any moment.

'It will be finished if it rains,' said Usha. And it did rain that night—rain mingled with sleet and hail. It rattled and swished on the corrugated tin roof; but in the morning the sun came out. I walked up the road without really expecting to see the flower again. And Usha had been right. The flower had disappeared in the storm. But two other buds, unnoticed by us the day before, had opened. It was as though two tiny stars had fallen to earth in the night.

I did not see Usha that day; but the following day, when we met on the road, I showed her the fresh blossoms. And they were still there, two days later, when I passed by; but so were two goats, grazing on the short grass and thorny thickets of the slope. I had no idea if they were partial to these particular flowers, but I did know that goats would eat almost anything and I was taking no chances.

Scrambling up the steep slope, I began to shoo them away. One goat retreated; but the other lowered his horns, gave me a baleful look, and refused to move. It reminded me a little of my grandfather's pet goat who had once pushed a visiting official into a bed of nasturtiums; so I allowed discretion to be the better part of valour, and backed away.

Just then, Usha came along and, sizing up the situation, came to the rescue. She unfurled her pretty blue umbrella and advanced on the goat shouting at it in goat language. (She had her own goats at home.) The beast retreated, and the flowers (and my own dignity) were saved.

As the days grew warmer, the flowers faded and finally disappeared. I forgot all about them, and so did Usha. There were lessons and exams for her to worry about, and rent and electricity bills to occupy a freelance writer's thoughts.

The months passed, summer and autumn came and went, with their own more showy blooms; and in no time at all, winter returned with cold winds

blowing from all directions.

One day I heard Usha calling to me from the hillside. I looked up and saw her standing behind a little cluster of golden star-shaped flowers—not, perhaps, as spectacular as Wordsworth's field of golden daffodils but, all the same, an enchanting sight for one who had played a small part in perpetuating their existence.

Where there had been one flowering plant, there were now several. Usha and I speculated on the prospect of the entire hillside being covered with the flowers in a few years' time.

I still do not know the botanical name for the little flower. I can't remember long Latin names anyway. But Usha tells me that she has seen it growing near her father's village, on the next mountain, and that the hill people call it 'Basant', which means spring.

Although I am just a little disappointed that we are not, after all, the discoverers of a new species, this is outweighed by our pleasure in knowing that the flower flourishes in other places. May it multiply!

Our Insect Musicians

WHEN THE monsoon with its magic touch brings life and greenness to rock and earth and withered tree, our insect musicians are roused to their greatest activity. The whole air at dusk seems to tinkle and murmur to their music. To the shrilling of the grasshoppers is added the staccato notes of the crickets, while in the grass myriads of lesser artistes provide a medley of sounds.

As musicians the cicadas are in a class of their own. There are many species of the cicada in India, most of them forest dwellers. All through the hot weather their screaming chorus rings through the forest, while a shower of rain, far from damping their ardour, only rouses them to a defeating crescendo of effort.

The ancient Greeks knew the cicada well. They called him tetix, and appreciated his music so much that they kept him captive in a cage to hear him sing. Well, there is no accounting for tastes!

Only the males were chosen—for the females, as with most insect musicians, are completely dumb. This moved one chauvinistic Greek poet (Xenarchos, I think) to exclaim: 'Happy are the cicadas, for they have voiceless wives!'

The music of the cicadas varies. Each species plays its distinctive tune. Their music-producing instruments are so complex that they must be regarded amongst the most remarkable sound-producing organs in the animal kingdom.

The underside of a cicada's body carries a pair of flaps, each of which covers an oval membrane which looks like the head of a drum, set in a solid rim of the body

wall. The cicada does not beat his drums. They are set into intense vibration by a great pair of muscles attached to them from within the body. The sound is produced by the vibration of the drums, while the whole abdomen, which is practically hollow, helps to increase or diminish the sound, according to the position of the covering flaps. Simple, isn't it? To be truthful, I find it extremely complicated, and am able to describe the process only by consulting the notes of S. H. Prater, one-time curator of the Bombay Natural History Society.

Let it be added that the female carries these structures in a modified form, but, as she has no muscles to bring them into play, she is unable to use them. This is why she must remain silent while her spouse shrieks away. I would change the line from that Greek poet and say instead: 'Pity the female cicadas, for they have singing husbands!'

Perhaps the most familiar and homely of insect singers are the crickets. I won't go into detail over how the cricket produces its music, except to say that its louder notes are produced by a rapid vibration of the wings, the right wing usually working over the left, the edge of one acting on the file of the other to produce a shrill, long-sustained note.

One of the best-known crickets is a large black fellow who lives underground and rarely comes out by day, except when the rains flood him out of his burrow. But when night falls, he sits on his doorstep and pours out his soul in a strident song. This cricket's name is as impressive as his sound—*Brachytrupes portentosus*.

The mole-cricket is a genius by itself. Mole-crickets are tillers of the soil. They use their powerful forelimbs for shovelling up the earth and their hard heads for butting into it. Notwithstanding its earthy occupations, the mole-cricket is sometimes moved to creating music. But as he repeats his note, a solemn deep-toned chirp, about a hundred times a minute, the performance can be monotonous.

In India, the cone-headed katydids are probably the most notable performers.

Katydids are trim, slender grasshopper-like insects, much in evidence in the fresh green grass of the monsoon. In the fields the loud shrill notes of the males may be heard both by day and by night. Sometimes one of them comes into the house and treats its occupants to a sudden outburst of high-pitched fiddling. His song rises in pitch as the performer warms to his work. In a room it can be quite deafening; and the sound is always difficult to locate—it seems to come from everywhere.

Finally we come to the tree crickets, a band of willing artistes who commence their performance at dusk. Their sounds are familiar, but it is difficult to see the musicians. Delicate pale green creatures with transparent green wings, they are hard to find among the foliage. And a tap on the bush or leaf on which they sit will put an immediate end to the performance.

Presumably the males sing in order to attract their more silent females. The music advertises the presence of the male, just as in other creatures it is colour or smell that does the job. After a performance, the female can sometimes be seen feeding off a sweet nectar that is contained in a cavity just behind the male's wings. Well, even the human male seeks to please his sweetheart with the offer of chocolates. And if music be the food of love, play on!

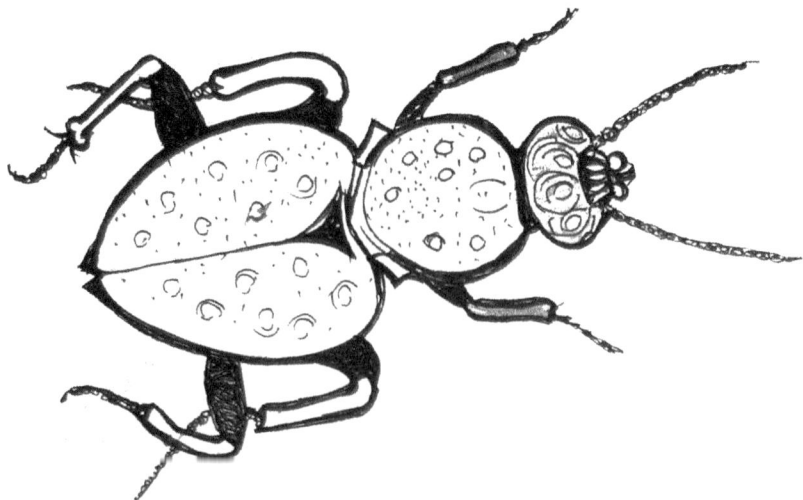

Birds of the Night

HAVING FOR a number of years suffered from rather poor vision, I am not the most eagle-eyed of birdwatchers. But, like many who don't see too well, I have good powers of hearing, awakening in the night at the squeak of a mouse or the fluttering of a moth against the window pane. And when, at times, sleep is elusive, I can lie awake and derive pleasure from the sounds and calls of those birds who live largely by night.

Not that all bird-calls are pleasing to the ear. The hawk-cuckoo semitones until one begins to think that the performer must surely burst. But the brainfever bird never bursts. Its cry is repeated for hours at a stretch.

He is a hot-weather bird who haunts the groves and gardens in almost all parts of the country, his range extending from the Himalayan foothills to Cape Comorin. Only Assam and Punjab appear to be free from the attentions of this cuckoo.

Another cuckoo, the common Indian cuckoo, has quite a pleasant note, which may be rendered by the words 'wherefore, wherefore,' with quite a musical cadence. It begins to call about two hours before sunset, and continues through the night until the morning hours. It is usually silent during the middle of the day, when presumably, it rests its vocal chords.

There is a third night-loving cuckoo, the koel, who, like the brainfever bird, is not very popular with those who try to sleep within hearing distance. His 'ku-oo' grows more strident with each successive rise in scale until sleep becomes almost impossible for anyone in the vicinity. Cunningham described it as a highly pitched, trisyllabic cry, repeated many times in ascending, as Douglas Dewar writes, 'the jaded dweller in the plains, uttering strange oaths, rushes for his gun and seeks out the disturber of his slumber.' But the clamour breaks off abruptly, and the sleeper returns to bed, rejoicing in the thought that the wretched bird has choked itself. And it is just then that the bird begins all over again!

Well, there are the nightjars, not much to look at, although their large, lustrous eyes gleam uncannily in the light of a lamp. But their sounds are distinctive. The breeding call of the Indian nightjar resembles the sound of a stone skimming over the surface of a frozen pond; it can be heard for a considerable distance. Another species utters a loud grating call which, when close at hand, sounds exactly like a whiplash cutting the air. 'Horsfield's nightjar' makes a noise similar to that made by striking a plank with a hammer.

During the day the bird spends long hours sitting motionless on the ground, where it is practically invisible, only springing into life when an intruder approaches. It is also called the 'Goatsucker' because of its huge mouth and the legend spread in many countries that it feeds from the udders of cows and goats. Because of this erroneous belief, it is considered a bird of ill omen. Night-flying insects, such as moths and beetles, are its preferred meals.

I must not forget the owls, those most celebrated of night birds, much maligned by those who fear the night. Most owls have very pleasant calls. The little jungle owlet has a note which is both mellow and musical. One misguided writer has likened its call to a motorcycle starting up, but this is a libel. If only motorcycles sounded like the jungle owl, the world would be a more peaceful place to live and sleep in.

Then there is the little scops owl, who speaks only in monosyllables, occasionally saying 'wow' softly but with great deliberation. He will continue to say 'wow' at intervals of about a minute, for several hours throughout the night.

Probably the most familiar of Indian owls is the spotted owlet, a noisy bird who pours forth a volley of chuckles and squeaks in the early evening and at intervals all night. Towards sunset, I watch the owlets emerge from their holes one after another. Before coming out, each puts out a queer little round head with staring eyes. After they have emerged they usually sit very quietly for a time as though only half awake. Then, all of a sudden, they begin to chuckle, finally breaking out in a torrent of chattering. Having in this way 'psyched' themselves into the right frame of mind, they spread their short, rounded wings and sail off for the night's hunting.

With the window open at night there is always something to listen to, the mellow whistle of the little owlet, the honk of a nightjar, the rustle of porcupines, the call of a barking deer. Sometimes, if I am lucky, I see the moon come up over Landour, and two tall deodars silhouetted against it.

To See a Tiger

MR KISHORE, my neighbour, drove me out to the forest rest house in his jeep, told me he'd be back in two days, and left me in the jungle. The caretaker of the rest house, a retired Indian Army corporal, made me a cup of tea.

'You have come to see the animals, sir?'

'Yes,' I said, looking around the clearing in front of the house, where a few domestic fowls scrabbled in the dust. 'Will I have to go far?'

'This is the best place, sir,' said the caretaker. 'See, the river is just below.'

A stream of clear mountain water ran through a shady glade of sal and shisham trees about 50 yards from the house.

'The animals come at night,' said the caretaker. 'You can sit in the veranda, with a cup of tea, and watch them. You must be very quiet, of course.'

'Will I see a tiger?' I asked. 'I've come to see a tiger.'

'Perhaps the tiger will come, sir,' said the caretaker with a tolerant smile. 'He will do his best, I am sure.'

He made me a simple lunch of rice and lentils, flavoured with a mango pickle. I spent the afternoon with a book taken from the rest house bookshelf. The small library hadn't been touched for over 20 years, and I had to make my choice from Marie Corelli, P. C. Wren, and early Wodehouse. I plumped for a

Wodehouse—*Love among the Chickens*. A peacock flaunted its tail feathers on the lawn, but I was not distracted. I had seen plenty of peacocks.

When it grew dark, I took up my position in the veranda, on an old cane chair. Bhag Singh, the caretaker, brought me dinner on a brass thali (tray), with two different vegetables in separate katoris (brass bowls). The chapaties came in relays, brought hot from the kitchen by Bhag Singh's ten-year-old son. Then, sustained by more tea, sweet and milky, I began my vigil. It took an hour for Bhag Singh's family to settle down for the night in their outhouse. Their pi-dog stood outside, barking at me for half an hour, before he too fell asleep. The moon came up over the foothills, and the stream could be seen quite clearly.

And then a strange sound filled the night air. Not the roar of a tiger, nor the sawing of a leopard, but a rising crescendo of noise—wurk, wurk, wurk—issuing from the muddy banks near the stream. All the frogs in the jungle seemed to have gathered there that night. They must have been having a sort of an old boys' reunion, because everyone seemed to have something to say for himself. The speeches continued for about an hour. Then the meeting broke up, and silence returned to the forest.

A jackal slunk across the clearing. A puff of wind brushed through the trees. I was almost asleep when a cicada burst into violent music in a nearby tree. I started, and stared out at the silver, moon-green stream; but no animals came to drink that night.

The next evening Bhag Singh offered to sit up with me. He placed a charcoal burner on the veranda, and topped it with a large basin of tea.

'Whenever you feel sleepy, sir, I'll give you a glass of tea.'

Did we hear a panther—or was it someone sawing wood? The sounds are similar, in the distance. The frogs started up again. The old boys must have brought their wives along this time, because instead of speeches there was general conversation, exactly like the natter of a cocktail party.

By morning I had drunk over fifteen cups of tea. Out of respect for my grandfather, a pioneer tea planter in India, I did not complain. Bhag Singh made me an English breakfast—toast, fried eggs, and more tea.

The third night passed in much the same way, except that Bhag Singh's son stayed up with us and drank his quota of tea.

In the morning, Mr Kishore came for me in his jeep. 'Did you see anything?'

'A jackal,' I said.

'Never mind, you'll have better luck next time. Of course, the jungles aren't what they used to be. . .'

I said goodbye to Bhag Singh, and got into the jeep.

We had gone barely a hundred yards along the forest road when Mr Kishore brought the jeep to a sudden, jolting halt.

Right in the middle of the road, about 30 yards in front of us, stood a magnificent full-grown tiger.

The tiger didn't roar. He didn't even snarl. But he gave us what appeared to be a quick, disdainful glance, and then walked majestically across the road and into the jungle.

'What luck!' exclaimed Mr Kishore. 'You can't complain now, can you? You've seen your tiger!'

'Yes,' I said, 'three sleepless nights, and I've seen it in broad daylight!'

'Very considerate of the tiger,' laughed Mr Kishore, and drove on.

Great Trees I Have Known

LIVING FOR many years in a cottage at 7000 feet in the Garhwal Himalayas, I was fortunate in having a big window that opened out on the forest, so that the trees were almost within my reach. Had I jumped, I should have landed quite safely in the arms of an oak or a chestnut.

The incline of the hill was such that my first-floor window opened on what must, I suppose, have been the second floor. I never made the jump, but the big langurs, silver-red monkeys with long swishing tails, often leapt from the trees on to the corrugated tin roof and made enough noise to disturb the bats sleeping in the space between the roof and ceiling.

Standing on its own was a walnut tree, and truly, this was a tree for all seasons. In winter the branches were bare but they were smooth and straight and round like the arms of a woman in a painting by Jamini Roy. In spring each branch produced a hard bright spear of new leaf. By midsummer the entire tree was in leaf, and towards the end of monsoon the walnuts, encased in their green jackets, had reached maturity.

Then the jackets began to split, revealing the hard brown shell of the walnuts. Inside the shell was the nut itself. Look closely at the nut and you will notice that it is shaped rather like the human brain. No wonder the ancients prescribed walnuts for headaches!

Every year the tree gave me a basket of walnuts. But last year the walnuts were disappearing one by one, and I was at a loss to know who had been taking them. Could it have been Biju, the milkman's son? He was an inveterate tree climber. But he was usually to be found on oak trees, gathering fodder for his cows. He told me that his cows liked oak leaves but did not care for walnuts. He admitted that they had relished my dahlias, which they had eaten the previous week, but he denied having fed them walnuts.

It wasn't the woodpecker. He was out there every day, knocking furiously against the bark of the tree, trying to prise an insect out of a narrow crack. He was strictly non-vegetarian and none the worse for it.

One day I found a fat langur sitting in the walnut tree. I watched him for some time to see if he was going to help himself to the nuts, but he was only sunning himself. When he thought I wasn't looking, he came down and ate the geraniums; but he did not take any walnuts.

The walnuts had been disappearing early in the morning while I was still in bed. So one morning I surprised everyone, including myself, by getting up before sunrise. I was just in time to catch the culprit climbing out of the walnut tree.

She was an old woman who sometimes came to cut grass on the hillside. Her face was as wrinkled as the walnuts she had been helping herself to. In spite of her age, her arms and legs were sturdy. When she saw me, she was as swift as a civet cat in getting out of the tree.

'And how many walnuts did you gather today, Grandmother?' I asked.

'Only two,' she said with a giggle, offering them to me on her open palm. I accepted one of them. Encouraged, she climbed back into the tree and helped herself to the remaining nuts. It was impossible to object. I was taken up in admiration of

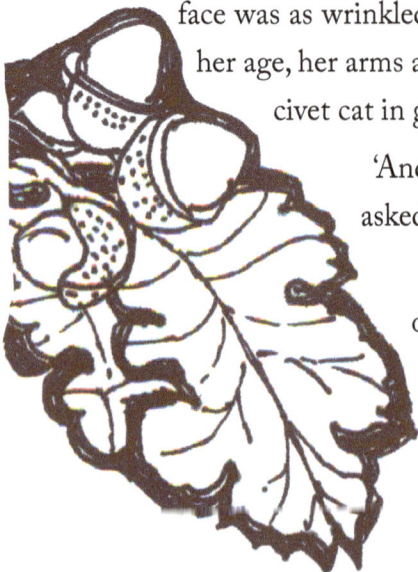

her agility in the tree. She must have been about 60, and I was a mere 45, but I knew I would never be climbing trees again.

To the victor the spoils!

Horse chestnuts are inedible, even the monkeys throw them away in disgust. Once, on passing beneath a horse chestnut tree, a couple of chestnuts bounced off my head. Looking up, I saw that they had been dropped on me by a couple of mischievous rhesus monkeys.

The tree itself is a friendly one, especially in summer when it is in full leaf. The least breath of wind makes the leaves break into conversation, and their rustle is a cheerful sound, unlike the sad notes of pine trees in the wind. The spring flowers look like candelabra, and when the blossoms fall they carpet the hillside with their pale pink petals.

We pass now to my favourite tree, the deodar. In Garhwal and Kumaon it is called dujar or devdar, in Jaunsar and in parts of Himachal it is known as the kelu kelon. It is also identified with the cedar of Lebanon (the cones are identical), although the deodar's needles are slightly longer and more bluish. Trees, like humans, change with their environment. Several persons familiar with the deodar at Indian hill stations, when asked to point it out in London's Kew Gardens, indicated the cedar of Lebanon; and shown a deodar, declared that they had never seen such a tree in the Himalayas!

We shall stick to the name deodar, which comes from the Sanskrit deva-daru (divine tree). It is a sacred tree in the Himalayas; not worshipped, nor protected in the way that a peepul is in the plains, but sacred in that its timber has always been used in temples, for doors, windows, walls and even roofs. Quite frankly, I would just as soon worship the deodar as worship anything, for in the beauty and majesty it represents Creation in its most noble aspect.

No one who has lived amongst deodar would deny that it is the most godlike of Himalayan trees. It stands erect, dignified; and though in a strong wind it may hum and sigh and moan, it does not bend to the wind. The snow slips softly from its resilient branches. In the spring the new leaves are a tender green, while during monsoon the tiny young cones spread like blossoms in the dark green folds of the branches. The deodar thrives in the rain and enjoys the company of its own kind. Where one deodar grows, there will be others. Isolate a young tree and it will often pine away.

The great deodar forests are found along the upper reaches of the Bhagirathi valley and the Tons in Garhwal; and in Himachal and Kashmir, along the Chenab and the Jhelum, and also on the Kishenganga; it is at its best between 7000 and 9000 feet. I had expected to find it on the upper reaches of the Alaknanda, but could not find a single deodar along the road to Badrinath. That particular valley seems hostile to trees in general, and deodar in particular.

The timber of these trees, which is unaffected by extremes of climate, was always highly prized for house building, and in the villages of Jaunsar Bawar, finely carved doors and windows are a feature of the timbered dwellings. Many of the quaint old bridges over the Jhelum in Kashmir are supported on pillars fashioned from whole deodar trees; some of these bridges are more than 500 years old.

To return to my own trees, I went among them often, acknowledging their presence with a touch of my hand against their trunks—the walnut's smooth and polished; the pine's patterned and whorled; the oak's rough, gnarled, full of experience. The oak had been there the longest, and the wind had bent his upper branches and twisted a few, so that he looked shaggy and undistinguished. It is a good tree for the privacy of birds, its crooked branches spreading out with no particular effect; and sometimes the tree seems uninhabited until there is a whirring sound, as of a helicopter approaching, and a party of long-tailed blue magpies stream across the forest glade.

After the monsoon, when the dark red berries had ripened on the hawthorn, this pretty tree was visited by green pigeons, the kokla birds of Garhwal, who clambered upside down among the fruit-laden twigs. And during winter, a white-capped redstart perched on the bare branches of the wild pear tree and whistled cheerfully. He had come down from higher places to winter in the garden.

The pines grow on the next hill—the chir, the Himalayan blue pine, and the long-leaved pine—but there is a small blue pine a little way below the cottage, and sometimes I sit beneath it to listen to the wind playing softly in its branches.

Explore the history and mythology of almost any Indian tree, and you will find that at some period of our civilization it has held an important place in the minds and hearts of the people of this land.

During the rains, when the neem pods fall and are crushed underfoot, they give out a strong refreshing aroma which lingers in the air for days. This is because the neem gives out more oxygen than most trees. When the ancient herbalists held that the neem was a great purifier of the air, and that its leaves, bark and sap had medicinal qualities, they were quite right, for the neem is still used in medicine today.

From the earliest times it was connected with the gods who protect us from disease. Some castes regarded the tree as sacred to Sitala, the smallpox goddess. When children fell ill, a branch of the neem was waved over them. The tree is said to have sprung from the nectar of the gods, and people still chew the leaves as a means of purification, both spiritual and physical.

The tree is also connected with the sun, as in the story of neem-barak, 'The Sun in the Neem Tree'. The Sun God invited to dinner a man of the Bairagi tribe whose rules forbade him to eat except by daylight. Dinner was late, and as darkness fell, the Bairagi feared he would have to go hungry. But Suraj Narayan, the Sun God, descended from a neem tree and continued shining till dinner was over.

Why have so many trees been held sacred, not only in India but the world over?

To early man they were objects of awe and wonder. The mystery of their growth, the movement of their leaves and branches, the way they seemed to die and then come to life again in spring, the sudden growth of the plant from the seed, all these happenings appeared as miracles—as indeed they are! And because of the wonderful growth of a tree, people began to suppose that it was occupied by spirits, and devotion to a tree became devotion to the spirit or tree god who occupied it.

In *Puck of Pook's Hill*, Kipling wove some wonderful stories, around Puck, the tree spirit, and the sacred trees of Old England—oak, ash and thorn: 'I came into England with Oak, Ash, and Thorn, and when Oak, Ash and Thorn are gone, I shall go too.'

Among the Gonds of central India, before a man cut a tree he had to beg its pardon for the injury he was about to inflict on it. He would not shake a tree at night because the tree spirit was asleep and might be disturbed. When a tree had to be felled, the Gonds would pour ghee on the stump, saying: 'Grow thou out of this, O Lord of the Forest, grow into a hundred shoots! May we grow with a thousand shoots.'

The beautiful mahua is a forest tree held sacred by a number of tribes. Early on the wedding morning, before he goes to fetch his bride, the Bagdi bridegroom

goes through a mock marriage with a mahua tree. He embraces it and daubs it with vermilion, his right wrist is bound to it with thread, and after he is released from the tree the thread is used to attach a bunch of mahua leaves to his wrist.

There is a beautiful tradition connected with the sal tree. It is said that at the time of the Buddha's birth, his mother stretched out her hand to take hold of a branch of the sal and was delivered. Sal trees are also said to have rendered homage to the Buddha at his death, letting fall on him their flowers out of season, and bending their branches to shade him.

Special respect is paid to trees growing near the graves of Muslim saints. Near the tomb of a famous saint, Musa Sohag, at Ahmedabad, there used to be a large old champa tree—perhaps it is still there—the branches of which were hung with glass bangles. Those anxious to have children came and offered bangles to the saint—the number of bangles depending on the means of the supplicant. If the saint favoured a wish, the champa tree 'snatched up the bangles and wore them on its arms'.

Another spectacular tree which has its place in our folklore is the dhak, or palash, which gave its name to the battlefield of Plassey. It has the habit of dropping its leaves when it flowers, the upper and outer branches standing out in sprays of scarlet and orange. The flowers are sometimes used to dye the powder scattered at Holi, the spring festival; and the wood, said to contain the seed of fire, is used in lighting the Holi bonfire. Legend tells us that the Sun God aimed an arrow at the earth, and that it took root and became the palasa tree.

The babul (or keekar) is not very impressive to look at but it will grow almost anywhere in the plains, and there are a number of old beliefs associated with it. For instance, you can cure fever and headache at a babul tree if you tie seven cotton threads from your left big toe to your head, and from your head to a branch of the tree. Then you must embrace the trunk seven times. Try it sometime. You will be so busy tying threads that you will forget you ever had a headache! And there are no after-effects.

Another belief concerning the babul is that if you water it regularly for thirteen days, you acquire control over the spirit who occupies it. There is a story about a man at Saharanpur who did this, and when he died and his corpse was taken away for cremation, no sooner was his pyre lit than he got up and walked away!

In the folklore of India, the mango is the 'wish-fulfilling tree'. When you want to make a wish on a mango tree, shut your eyes and get someone to lead you to the tree; then rub mango blossoms in your hands, and make your wish. The favour granted lasts only for a year, and the charm must be performed again at the next flowering of the tree. In the spring, the young leaves and buds symbolize the darts of Manmatha, or Kamadeva, God of Love.

Another 'wishing tree', the kalp-vriksha, is an enormous old mulberry that is still cared for at Joshimath in Garhwal. It is said to be the tree beneath which the great Sankaracharya often meditated during his sojourn in the Himalayas. Judging by its girth, it might well be over a thousand years old.

Whole forests have been held sacred, such as that in Berar which was dedicated to a particular temple; no one dared to buy or cut the trees. The sacred groves near Mathura, where Lord Krishna sported as a youth, were also protected for centuries. But now, alas, even the hallowed groves are disappearing, making way for the demands of an ever-increasing population. A pity, because every human needs a tree of his own. Even if you do not worship the tree spirit, you can love the tree.

The Charm of Elephants

EVERYONE LIKES elephants. Go where you will, you won't hear a harsh word against these outsize animals, who combine power with gentleness, a childish sulkiness with good humour, and great girth with a ballet dancer's poise.

Dickens wrote that the elephant employed the worst tailor in the world, but Dickens wasn't a poet. 'An eye like the antelope's, a waist like the lion's, and a gait like the elephant's'—these, according to an ancient Indian sage, were the outstanding characteristics of ideal femininity.

The elephant is a firm favourite in Hindu and Buddhist folklore, and in India there is a god called Ganesh who has an elephant's head. How he got his head is rather a long story, but Ganesh is the god of good beginnings. The businessman who opens a new ledger, the writer who starts a new book, and the traveller about to set out on a journey, all invoke the blessings of Ganesh.

Elephants are not sacred, like cows, but they are held in great affection, and no animal has names as pretty as those given to an elephant by his mahout, or keeper. Necklace of Beauty, Lily, Rose, Jasmine, Lotus, Garland of Marigolds, Silver Star, Black Snake and Golden One: these are only a few of the names elephants receive.

But why are these animals held in such great esteem?

The reasons are not hard to find. Elephants are intelligent, hard-working and obedient. They like men, and adjust themselves quickly to the ways of men (I am alluding to the Indian, and not the African elephant; the latter's fine ivory tusks have made him a hunted, tragic creature). Elephants return affection, they are nimble and strong, and they are wonderful to look at.

I don't think you will find elephants in the streets of Nairobi, but you will frequently see them in the streets of Delhi or Colombo or Rangoon. They are patient with traffic, and co-exist wonderfully well with buses, cars, horse-drawn buggies, cyclists and bullock carts.

Though there are still many wild elephants in India, they can almost be classified as domestic animals, for they feel quite at home with human beings. Wild elephants are usually rounded up by tame elephants, who exert an immediate civilizing effect on their brethren! But elephants can be unpredictable. I have seen a tame elephant rescue marooned villagers from an island in the middle of a flooded river; yet on another occasion this same elephant went berserk and smashed up the village post office.

Elephants are noted for their nimbleness, and in parts of Assam there is a belief that wild elephants sometimes assemble together to dance. A mahout once told me that he had come upon a large forest clearing, the floor beaten smooth and hard, 'It was an elephant nautch-khana,' he said. A ballroom!

While there is nothing to substantiate this story, it is true that elephants (like stout people, who are often light dancers) are very buoyant on both land and water. There is no reason why they shouldn't dance, and I am quite happy to go along with the quaint belief that elephants meet by moonlight in their forest ballrooms to dance their reels and quadrilles. The music they produce with their trunks is no better or worse than the music of a bagpipe.

'There are many footsteps in the footprint of an elephant,' is an old Indian saying—for in former times it was only rajas who could afford to keep their own elephants, and rajas had large retinues. In old forts and palaces throughout India

there are special elephant paths and high-arched elephant gates, through which the state elephants once marched.

On ceremonial occasions an elephant is still 'dressed'. He is made to lie down by his mahout and then he is washed like a child, raising his head or leg at a word, while the mahout's small son climbs about the animal's huge bulk and scrubs him with a brick. The elephant sometimes plays with the soapy water, blowing clouds of vapour from his trunk.

When the washing is over, he is dressed. First the forehead, trunk and ears are painted in bold patterns; there are mahouts who are very skilful in this work. Then the howdah is girt on with cotton ropes, which do not chafe the skin. The howdah, too, is lavishly decorated, sometimes with gold and silver ornaments.

The elephant goes through all this with great patience, but sometimes, when all is ready, he will suddenly fling a bunch of leaves and fodder over his back, to give his mahout a little extra work before the parade begins.

At one time elephants were taken by ship from Calcutta to Chittagong, down on the Bay of Bengal. They were needed in Chittagong to help in piling timber, a job which they performed with neatness and precision.

A steamer with forty elephants aboard sailed down the Hooghly, anchoring for the night in a calm sea off Saugor Island. The ship's transport officer did not know that elephants are among the most restless creatures alive, always in motion. At first the crew said it was a ground swell that made the ship roll so much, but they soon found that it was due to the movements of the elephants.

The great beasts had discovered that by swaying to and fro, all together, they could produce a pleasing rhythmic motion. So, they rolled and swung in unison, till the ship was in danger of rolling over with them.

The mahouts were hurried down into the hold, and, each seated on an elephant, made the creatures break step. The swaying of the ship ceased; but another difficulty was encountered in carrying fodder down the narrow passageway between the elephants.

They would allow a laden coolie to proceed some way, and then one of their number, quietly mischievous, would trip the man over with its trunk, while the others snatched away the bundles of grass. Finally the coolies had to crawl over the backs of the elephants to get to the far end of the hold.

When the ship arrived in port there was no wharf, and the animals had to swim and wade through a mile of water from the anchorage to the shore. The first elephant was lowered from the deck to the water, with his mahout on his neck, and a Lascar seaman clinging to the chain to let go the swivel. The man let go too soon, the elephant fell with a mighty splash, while the suddenly released chain shot the astonished seaman like a bolt from a catapult into the sea some 50 yards away.

But no one came to any harm, and the elephants made their way safely ashore. To anyone who may have been standing on the shore it must have been a most unusual and awe-inspiring sight, as those forty great elephants rose out of the sea, like monsters of the deep, to walk majestically through the surf towards new forests and a new life.

The Friendship of Flowers

THE LITTLE rose begonia: it has a glossy chocolate leaf, a pretty rose-pink flower. It grows and flowers in my bedroom—almost all the year round. What more can one ask for?

Some plants become friends. Most garden flowers are fair-weather friends; gone in the winter when times are difficult up here in the mountains. Those who stand by you in adversity—plant or human—are your true friends; there aren't many around, so cherish them and take care of them in all seasons.

A loyal plant friend is the variegated ivy that has spread all over my bedroom wall. My small bedroom-cum-study gets plenty of light and sun, and when the windows are open, cool breeze from the mountains floats in, rustling the leaves of the ivy. (This breeze can turn into a raging blizzard in winter—on one occasion, even blowing the roof away—but right now, it's just a zephyr, gentle and balmy.) Ivy plants seem to like my room, and this one, which I brought up from Dehra, took an instant liking to my desk and walls, so that I now have difficulty keeping it from trailing over my typewriter when I am at work.

I like to take in other people's sick or discarded plants and nurse or cajole them back to health. This has given me a bit of a reputation as a plant doctor. Actually, all I do is give an ailing plant a quiet corner where it can rest and recuperate from whatever ails it—they have usually been ill-treated in some way. Plant abuse, no less! And it's wonderful how quickly a small tree or plant will recover if given a little encouragement.

I rescued a dying asparagus fern from the portals of the Savoy Hotel, and now, six months later, its strong feathery fronds have taken over most of one window, so that I have no need of curtains. Nandu, the owner of Savoy, now wants his fern back.

Maya Banerjee's sick geranium, never allowed to settle in one place—hence its stunted appearance—has, within a fortnight of being admitted to my plant ward, burst forth in such an array of new leaf and flower that I'm afraid it might pull a muscle or strain a ligament from too much activity.

Should I return these and other plants when they have fully recovered? I don't think they want to go back. And I should hate to see them suffering relapses on being returned to their former abodes. So I tell the owners that their plants need monitoring for a while. (Perhaps, if I sent in doctor's bills, the demands for their return would not be so strident?)

Loyalty in plants, as in friends, must be respected and rewarded. If dandelions show a tendency to do well on the steps of the house, then that is where they shall be encouraged to grow. If a sorrel is happier on the window sill than on the hillside, then I shall let it stay, even if it means the window won't close properly. And if the hydrangea does better in my neighbour's garden than mine, then my neighbour shall be given the hydrangea. Among flower lovers, there must be no double standards: generosity, not greed; sugar, not spite.

And what of the rewards for me, apart from the soothing effect of fresh fronds and leaves at my place of work and rest? Well, the other evening I came home to find my room vibrating to the full-throated chorus of several crickets who had found the ivy to their liking. I thought they would keep me up all night with their music; but when I switched the light off, they immediately fell silent. So, crickets don't sing in the dark, I surmised, and switched the light on again. Once

more, I was treated to symphonic variations on a theme by Tchaikovsky.

There are other rewards—like unexpected companionship. The dandelion growing on my retaining wall, for instance. It asserts its right to be there, where practically nothing else will flourish. Without any care or nourishment, it survives and grows strong and upright. Pluck it if you will, but there's no uprooting it from that space between two stones where it is so firmly embedded.

The dandelion opens its petals to the first rays of the sun and closes when the sunlight fades. And it is called love's oracle because of the custom of blowing on its puffball of seeds to discover whether 'X loves me' or 'X loves me not'. I have always been able to regulate my breath so as to obtain the answer I wanted!

A good companion when the dandelion is not in bloom, is the poppy, while it lasts. A classic flower, it is extravagantly beautiful. The scarlet poppy is the most showy but I like the plain white one as it makes for such a pleasing contrast, a pattern of poppies, scarlet and white.

And then, of course, there's the trusted geranium. I can meditate upon a geranium. That is, I can spend a long time gazing at one. And as I can get geraniums to flower in my sunny bedroom, summer and winter, I have every opportunity to do so.

The geranium that has done best is the one I have grown in a large plastic bucket standing on the chest of drawers and facing the early morning sun. Here, protected from wind and rain (both of which are anathema to geraniums), this generous plant has made a great display, producing no less than eight florets of soft pink confetti. Pastel shades have always appealed to me. And there is something alluring about this sensual pink. Other shades are appealing too—the salmon pink, the cerise, the flaming red—but this pale pink is restful, intimate. From my bed or desk I can gaze at it, and have pleasant thoughts.

Fragrance to the Air

I WOULD be the last person to belittle a flower for its lack of fragrance, because there are many spectacular blooms such as the dahlia and the gladioli which have hardly any scent and yet make up for it with their colour and appearance. But it does happen that my own favourite flowers are those with a distinctive fragrance and these are the flowers I would have around me.

The rose, of course, is the world's favourite, a joy to all—even to babies, who enjoy taking them apart, petal by petal. But there are other, less spectacular, less celebrated blooms which have a lovely, sometimes elusive fragrance of their own.

I have a special fondness for antirrhinums—or snapdragons, as they are more commonly known. If I sniff hard at them, I don't catch any scent at all. They seem to hold it back from me. But if I walk past a bed of snapdragons, or even a single plant, the gentlest of fragrance is wafted towards me. If I stop and try to take it all in, it has gone again! I find this quite tantalizing, but it has given me a special regard for this modest flower.

Another humble, even old-fashioned flower, is the wallflower which obviously takes its name from the fact that it thrives on walls. I have seen wallflowers adorn a garden wall in an extravagant and delightful manner, making it a mountain of perfume. They are best grown so as to form dense masses which become literally solid with fiery flowers—blood-red, purple, yellow, orange or bronze, all sending a heady fragrance into the surrounding air.

Carnations, with their strong scent of cloves, are great showoffs. In India, the jasmine and the magnolia are both rather heady and overpowering. The honeysuckle too insists on making its presence known. A honeysuckle creeper flourished outside the window of my room in Mussoorie, and all through the summer its sweet, rather cloying fragrance drifted in through the open window. It was delightful at times, but at other times I had to close the window just so that I could give my attention to other, less intrusive smells—like the soft, sweet scent of petunias (another of my favourites) growing near the doorstep, and great bunches of sweet peas stacked in a bowl on my desk.

It is much the same with chrysanthemums and geraniums. The lemon geranium, for instance, is valued more for its fragrant leaves than for its rather indeterminate blue flowers. And I cannot truthfully say what ordinary mint looks like in flower. The refreshing fragrance of the leaves, when crushed, makes up for any absence of floral display. On the other hand, the multicoloured loveliness of dahlias is unaccompanied by any scent. Its greenery, when cut or broken, does have a faintly acrid smell, but that's about all.

Not all plants are good to smell. Some leaves, when crushed, will keep strong men at bay! During the monsoon in the plains, neem pods fall and are crushed underfoot, giving out a distinctive odour. Most people dislike the smell, but I find it quite refreshing.

Of course, one man's fragrance might well turn out to be another creature's bad smell. Geraniums, my grandmother insisted, kept snakes away because they couldn't stand the smell of the leaves. She surrounded her bungalow with pots of geraniums. As we never found a snake in the house, she may well have been right. But the evidence is purely circumstantial.

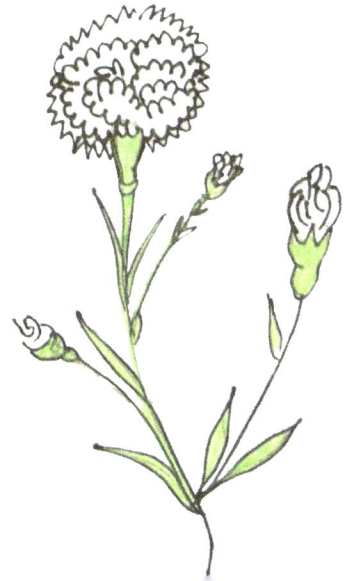

I suppose snakes like some smells, close to the ground, or by now they'd have taken to living in more elevated places. But, turning to a book on reptiles, I learnt from it that in the snake the sense of smell is rather dull. Perhaps it has an aversion to anything that it can smell—such as those aromatic geranium leaves!

Close to Mother Earth, there are many delightful smells, provided you avoid roadsides and freshly-manured fields. When I lie on summer grass in some Himalayan meadow, I am conscious of the many good smells around me— the grass itself, redolent of the morning's dew, bruised clover, wild violets, tiny buttercups and golden stars and strawberry flowers and many others I shall never know the names of.

And the earth itself. It smells different in different places. But its loveliest fragrance is known only when it receives a shower of rain. And then the scent of the wet earth rises as though it would give something beautiful back to the clouds. A blend of all the fragrant things that grow upon it.

The Garden of a Thousand Trees

NO ONE in his right mind would want to chop down a mango tree. Every mango tree, even if it grows wild, is generous with its juicy fruit, known sometimes as 'the nectar of the gods', and sometimes as the 'king of fruits'. You can eat ripe mangoes fresh from the tree; you can eat them in pickles or chutneys or jams; you can eat them flattened out and dried, as in aam papad; you can drink the juice with milk as in 'mango-fool'; you can even pound the kernel into flour and use it as a substitute for wheat. And there are over a hundred different varieties of the mango, each with its own distinctive flavour.

But in praising the fruit, let us not forget the tree, for it is one of the stateliest trees in India, its tall, spreading branches a familiar sight throughout the country, from the lower slopes of the Himalayas to Cape Comorin.

In Gujarat, on the night of the seventh of the month of Savan (July-August), a young mango tree is planted near the house and worshipped by the womenfolk to protect their children from disease. Sometimes a post of mango wood is set up when Ganesh is worshipped.

If you live anywhere in the plains of northern India, you will often have seen a grove of giant mango trees, sometimes appearing like an oasis in

the midst of the vast, flat countryside. Beneath the trees you may find a well and a small temple. It is here that the tired, dusty farmer sits down to rest and eat his midday chapati, following it with a draught of cold water from the well. If you join him and ask him who planted the mango grove, he will not be able to tell you; it was there when he was a boy, and probably when his father was a boy too. Some mango groves are very, very old.

Have you heard of the Garden of a Thousand Trees? Probably not. But you must have heard of the town of Hazaribagh in Bihar. Well, a huge mango grove containing over a thousand trees—some of which are still there—was known as hazari, and around these trees a village grew, spreading in time into the modern town of Hazaribagh, 'Garden of a Thousand Trees'. Anyway, that's the story you will hear from the oldest inhabitants of the town. And even today, the town is almost hidden in a garden of trees: mango and neem, sal and tamarind.

All are welcome in a mango grove. But during the mango season, when the trees are in fruit, you enter the grove at your own peril! At this time of the year it is watched over by a fierce chowkidar, whose business is to drive away any mischievous children who creep into the grove in the hope of catching him asleep and making off with a few juicy mangoes. The chowkidar is a busy man. Even before the mangoes ripen, he has to battle not only with the village urchins, but also with raiding parties of emerald-green parrots, who swarm all over the trees, biting deep into the green fruit. Sometimes he sits under a tree in the middle of the grove, pulling a rope which makes a large kerosene-tin rattle in the branches. He can try shouting too, but his voice can't compete with the screams of the

parrots. They wheel in circles round the grove and, spreading their tails, settle on the topmost branches.

Even when there are no mangoes, you will find parrots in the grove, because during their breeding season, their favourite nesting places are the holes in the gnarled trunks of old mango trees.

Other birds, including the blue jay and the little green coppersmith, favour the mango grove for the same reason. And sometimes you may spot a small owl peering at you from its hole halfway up the trunk of an old tree.

The Silk-Cotton Tree

Most of you, even if you do not play badminton, are familiar with a shuttlecock. Well, if you take a shuttlecock and paint it a bright crimson, you will get a fair idea of what the flower of the semul (or silk-cotton tree) looks like.

Now just imagine a tall, leafless tree covered with masses of crimson flowers, and you will know what this wonderful tree looks like in spring. There are few trees in the world that can compare with it in beauty and brilliance.

You may, of course, have seen a semul tree either in the jungle or along a tree-lined avenue in one of our cities. It is a good shade-tree, losing its leaves for only a brief period, just before it flowers. During the summer months you will find its seeds covered with white cotton, which is blown far and wide by the slightest breeze. This cotton is not suitable for spinning and weaving into cloth, but it is used for stuffing pillows and cushions.

Like most trees, the semul has its place in our folklore. Whenever the Murias, a forest tribe in Madhya Pradesh, found a village, their first act was to plant a semul tree at the centre of the site. There are others who use its wood to make

the posts around which couples walk at the marriage ceremony. Images of parrots fashioned from the wood of the semul are also hung in the marriage sheds, for the parrot represents the spirit of the forest.

Semul wood is very soft, and is sometimes used for making toys. Fishermen also use it to make floats for their nets. The seeds are valued as a nourishing food for cattle, while the gum from the bark is used in medicines by Ayurvedic doctors.

The semul is as remarkable for the colour and profusion of its flowers as for the large number of birds that visit it when it is in flower. Some birds come for the nectar which is found in the big, red flowers; some come in search of the thousands of drowned insects which lie at the bottom of the flower cups; some come because the soft wood of the tree can easily be hollowed out for a nesting site. Whatever the reason, from morning till night the tree is full of visitors.

Among those who visit the semul are a large number of crows, who come to have a few sips of the nectar before setting out on the day's mischief. There are mynas of various kinds, squabbling for the best seats. Barbets and bulbuls, king crows and koels, all join in the feasting. In addition to the birds, palm squirrels dart about from place to place, tossing their fluffy tails from side to side, and chattering noisily as they jostle each other on the branches. And all the time flowers are being constantly broken off, falling to the ground with soft thuds.

The rosy pastors or rose-coloured starlings are probably the most noticeable visitors to the semul tree. They come in flocks, not singly; their colour vies with that of the flowers; and they make such a racket that one thinks that a terrible riot is going on. But the pastors are not fighting, they are simply enjoying themselves.

Another inhabitant of the semul tree is the big Indian bee. This bee lives in huge nests, or combs, which are usually attached to the branches of the semul tree. The straight, horizontal branches of the semul are just right for supporting the huge combs, which can be as much as five feet in length and two and a half feet in width. The residents of the comb are of three kinds—the males or drones who do no work, the females who lay the eggs, and the workers who build the giant combs. These are permanent colonies, filled with honey or wax or pollen.

The sting of the big bee is painful and poisonous, especially in hot weather; but jungle tribes, such as the Kols and the Santals, have developed an immunity to the poison. They don't mind being stung. But strangers to the forests have been badly stung, and it is wise not to disturb these bees, for they will attack both man and beast with great ferocity.

There is the story of two shikaris who were resting between beats one hot May morning in a central Indian jungle. Overhead spread the crown of a tall semul tree with a dozen great combs of the big bee hanging from the branches. One of the shikaris unwisely lit a pipe. Up went the pipe smoke, and down came the bees! They were soon buzzing around the two shikaris, who beat an undignified retreat, running for over a mile across open country until they reached the safety of a river. They were so badly stung that they had to remain in the river for hours, up to their chins in water.

Guests Who Fly in from the Forest

WHEN MIST fills the Himalayan valleys, and heavy monsoon rain sweeps across the hills, it is natural for wild creatures to seek shelter. Any shelter is welcome in a storm—and sometimes my cottage in the forest is the most convenient refuge.

There is no doubt that I make things easier for all concerned by leaving most of my windows open—I am one of those peculiar people who like to have plenty of fresh air indoors—and if a few birds, beasts and insects come in too, they're welcome, provided they don't make too much of a nuisance of themselves.

I must confess that I did lose patience with a bamboo beetle who blundered in the other night and fell into the water jug. I rescued him and pushed him out of the window. A few seconds later he came whirring in again, and with unerring accuracy landed with a plop in the same jug. I fished him out once more and offered him the freedom of the night. But attracted no doubt by the light and warmth of my small sitting room, he came buzzing back, circling the room like a helicopter looking for a good place to land. Quickly I covered the water jug. He landed in a bowl of wild dahlias, and I allowed him to remain there, comfortably curled up in the hollow of a flower.

Sometimes, during the day, a bird visits me—a deep purple whistling-thrush, hopping about

on long dainty legs, peering to right and left, too nervous to sing. She perches on the windowsill, looking out at the rain. She does not permit any familiarity. But if I sit quietly in my chair, she will sit quietly on her windowsill, glancing quickly at me now and then just to make sure that I'm keeping my distance. When the rain stops, she glides away, and it is only then, confident in her freedom, that she bursts into full-throated song, her broken but haunting melody echoing down the ravine.

A squirrel comes sometimes, when his home in the oak tree gets waterlogged. Apparently he is a bachelor; anyway, he lives alone. He knows me well, this squirrel, and is bold enough to climb on to the dining table looking for titbits which he always finds, because I leave them there deliberately. Had I met him when he was a youngster, he would have learned to eat from my hand; but I have only been here a few months, I like it this way. I am not looking for pets: these are simply guests.

Last week, as I was sitting down at my desk to write a long-deferred article, I was startled to see an emerald green praying mantis sitting on my writing pad. He peered up at me with his protruberant glass bead eyes, and I stared down at him through my reading glasses. When I gave him a prod, he moved off in a leisurely way. Later I found him examining the binding of Whitman's *Leaves of Grass*; perhaps he had found a succulent bookworm. He disappeared for a couple of days, and then I found him on the dressing table, preening himself before the mirror. Perhaps I am doing him an injustice in assuming that he was preening. Maybe he thought he'd met another mantis and was simply trying to make contact. Anyway, he seemed fascinated by his reflection.

Out in the garden, I spotted another mantis, perched on the jasmine bush. Its arms were raised like a boxer's. Perhaps they're a pair, I thought, and went indoors and fetched my mantis and placed him on the jasmine bush, opposite his fellow insect. He did not like what he saw—no comparison with his own image!—and made off in a huff.

My most interesting visitor comes at night, when the lights are still burning—a tiny bat who prefers to fly in at the door, should it be open, and will use the window only if there's no alternative. His object in entering the house is to snap up the moths that cluster around the lamps.

All the bats I've seen fly fairly high, keeping near the ceiling as far as possible, and only descending to ear level (my ear level) when they must; but this particular bat flies in low, like a dive bomber, and does acrobatics amongst the furniture, zooming in and out of chair legs and under tables. Once, while careening about the room in this fashion, he passed straight between my legs.

Has his radar gone wrong, I wondered, or is he just plain crazy?

I went to my shelves of *Natural History* and looked up bats, but could find no explanation for this erratic behaviour. As a last resort, I turned to an ancient volume, Sterndale's *Indian Mammalia* (Calcutta, 1884), and in it, to my delight, I found what I was looking for—

a bat found near Mussoorie by Captain Hutton, on the southern range of hills at 5,500 feet; head and body, 1.4 inch; skims close to the ground, instead of flying high as bats generally do, Habitat, Jharipani, N. W. Himalayas.

Apparently the bat was rare even in 1884.

Perhaps I've come across one of the few surviving members of the species: Jharipani is only two miles from where I live. And I feel rather offended that modern authorities should have ignored this tiny bat; possibly they feel that it is already extinct. If so, I'm pleased to have rediscovered it. I am happy that it survives in my small corner of the woods. It may be a crazed little thing, but on solitary nights when you are in need of companionship, even a crazy bat is company.

No Room for a Leopard

I **FIRST** saw the leopard when I was crossing the small stream at the bottom of the hill. The ravine was so deep that for most of the day it remained in shadow. This encouraged many birds and animals to emerge from cover during the hours of daylight. Few people ever passed that way; only milkmen and charcoal burners from the surrounding villages. As a result the ravine had become a little haven for wildlife, one of the few natural sanctuaries left near Mussoorie.

Below my cottage was a forest of oak and maple and Himalayan rhododendron. A narrow path twisted its way down through the trees, over an open ridge where red sorrel grew wild, and then down steeply through a tangle of wild raspberries, creeping vines and slender rangal bamboo. At the bottom of the hill a path led onto a grassy verge surrounded by wild dogroses. The streams ran close by the verge, tumbling over smooth pebbles, over rock worn yellow with age, on its way to the plains and to the little Song river and finally to the sacred Ganga.

Nearly every morning, and sometimes during the day, I heard the cry of the barking deer. And in the evening walking through the forest, I disturbed parties of kaleej pheasants. The birds went gliding

into the ravines on open, motionless wings. I saw pine martens and a handsome red fox. I recognized the footprints of a bear.

As I had not come to take anything from the jungle the birds and animals soon grew accustomed to my face. Or possibly they recognized my footsteps. After some time, my approach did not disturb them. A spotted forktail, which at first used to fly away, now remained perched on a boulder in the middle of the stream while I got across by means of other boulders only a few yards away.

The langurs in the oak and rhododendron trees who would at first go leaping through the branches at my approach, now watched me with some curiosity as they munched up the tender green shoots of the oak. The young ones scuffled and wrestled like boys while their parents groomed each other's coats, stretching themselves out on the sunlit hillside—beautiful animals with slim waists and long sinewy legs and tails full of character. But one evening as I passed I heard them chattering in the trees and I was not the cause of their excitement.

As I crossed the stream and began climbing the hill, the grunting and chattering increased as though the langurs were trying to warn me of some hidden danger. A shower of pebbles came rattling down the steep hillside and I looked up to see a sinewy orange-gold leopard, poised on a rock about 20 feet above me.

It was not looking towards me but had its head thrust attentively forward in the direction of the ravine. It must have sensed my presence because it slowly turned its head and looked down at me. It seemed a little puzzled at my presence there, and when, to give myself courage, I clapped my hands sharply, the leopard sprang away into the thickets making absolutely no sound as it melted into the shadows. I had disturbed the animal in its quest for food. But a little later I heard the quickening cry of barking deer as it fled through the forest—the hunt was still on.

The leopard, like other members of the cat family, is nearing extinction in India and I was surprised to find one so close to Mussoorie. Probably the deforestation that had been taking place in the surrounding hills had driven the deer into this green valley and the leopard naturally had followed.

It was some weeks before I saw the leopard again although I was often made aware of its presence. A dry rasping cough sometimes gave it away. At times I felt certain that I was being followed. And once when I was late getting home I was startled by a family of porcupines running about in a clearing. I looked around nervously and saw two bright eyes staring at me from a thicket. I stood still, my heart banging away against my ribs. Then the eyes danced away and I realized they were only fireflies.

In May and June when the hills were brown and dry, it was always cool and green near the stream where ferns, maidenhair and long grasses continued to thrive.

One day I found the remains of a barking deer that had been partially eaten. I wondered why the leopard had not hidden the remains of his meal and decided that he had been disturbed while eating. Then, climbing the hill I met a party of shikaris resting beneath the oaks. They asked me if I had seen a leopard. I said I had not. They said they knew there was a leopard in the forest. Leopard skins, they told me, were selling in Delhi at over a thousand rupees each! Of course there was a ban on the export of its skins but they gave me to understand that there were ways and means. . .I thanked them for their information and moved on, feeling uneasy and disturbed.

The shikaris had seen the carcass of the deer and the leopard's pug marks and they kept coming to the forest. Almost every evening I heard their guns banging away for they were ready to fire at almost everything.

'There's a leopard about,' they told me. 'You should carry a gun.'

'I don't have one,' I said.

There were fewer birds to be seen and even the langurs had moved on. The red fox did not show itself and the pine martens who had earlier become bold, now dashed into hiding at my approach. The smell of one human is like the smell of any other.

I thought no more of the men. My attitude towards them was similar to the attitude of the denizens of the forest—they were men, unpredictable and to be avoided if possible.

One day after crossing the stream, I climbed Pari Tibba, a bleak, scrub-covered hill where no one lived. This was a stiff undertaking because there was no path to the top and I had to scramble up a precipitous rock-face with the help of rocks and roots which were apt to come away in my groping hand. But at the top was a plateau with a few pine trees, their upper branches catching the wind and humming softly. There I found the ruins of what must have been the first settlers—just a few piles of rubble now overgrown with weeds, sorrel, dandelion and nettles.

As I walked through the roofless ruins, I was struck by the silence that surrounded me, the absence of birds and animals, the sense of complete desolation. The silence was so absolute that it seemed to be shouting in my ears. But there was something else of which I was becoming increasingly aware—the strong feline odor of one of the cat family. I paused and looked about. I was alone. There was no movement of dry leaf or loose stone. The ruins were, for the most part, open to the sky. Their rotting rafters had collapsed and joined together to form a low passage like the entrance to a mine. This dark cavern seemed to lead down.

The smell was stronger when I approached this spot so I stopped again and waited there wondering if I had discovered the lair of the leopard, wondering if the animal was now at rest after a night's hunt. Perhaps it was crouched there in the dark, watching me, recognizing me, knowing me as a man who walked alone in the forest without a weapon. I like to think that he was there and that he knew me and that he acknowledged my visit in the friendliest way—by ignoring me altogether.

Perhaps I had made him confident—too confident, too careless, too trusting of the human in his midst. I did not venture any further. I did not seek physical contact or even another glimpse of that beautiful sinewy body, springing from rock to rock. It was his trust I wanted and I think he gave it to me. But did the leopard, trusting one man, make the mistake of bestowing his trust on others? Did I, by casting out all fear—my own fear and the leopard's protective fear—leave him defenceless?

Because next day, coming up the path from the stream, shouting and beating their drums, were the shikaris. They had a long bamboo pole across their shoulder and slung from the pole, feet up, head down, was the lifeless body of the leopard. It had been shot in the neck and in the head.

'We told you there was a leopard!' they shouted, in great good humour. 'Isn't he a fine specimen?'

'Yes,' I said, 'he was a beautiful leopard.'

I walked home through the silent forest. It was very silent, almost as though the birds and animals knew their trust had been violated.

I remembered the lines of a poem by D. H. Lawrence and as I climbed the steep and lonely path to my home, the words beat out their rhythm in my mind—'There was room in the world for a mountain lion and me'.

RUSKIN BOND is the author of numerous novellas, short-story collections and non-fiction books, many of them classics. Among them are *The Room on the Roof*, *A Flight of Pigeons*, *The Night Train at Deoli*, *Time Stops at Shamli*, *Landour Days*, *Rain in the Mountains* and *A Book of Simple Living*. He received the Sahitya Akademi Award in 1993, the Padma Shri in 1999 and the Padma Bhushan in 2014.

Ruskin lives in Landour, Mussoorie, with his extended family.

SHUBHADARSHINI SINGH was brought up in Kolkata and studied in Visva-Bharati, Shantiniketan. She has been an ad woman, a journalist and a film-maker. She shares Ruskin Bond's deep love for animals and wildlife and has been making his best stories into a series for television: *Ek Tha Rusty*.

Shubhadarshini runs an art gallery for Outsider Arts, and has had shows of her paintings in Delhi and Bhopal. She lives in Delhi with her husband, son and dogs.